I DIED SWALLOWING A GOLDFISH

AND OTHER LIFE LESSONS FROM THE MORGUE

J. KENT HOLLOWAY

Copyright © 2019 by J. Kent Holloway

Paperback ISBN: 978-0-578-60105-2

All rights reserved.

All Scripture quotations, unless otherwise indicated, are taken from the Holy Bible, New International Version®, NIV®. Copyright ©1973, 1978, 1984, 2011 by Biblica, Inc.™ Used by permission of Zondervan. All rights reserved worldwide. www.zondervan.com The "NIV" and "New International Version" are trademarks registered in the United States Patent and Trademark Office by Biblica, Inc.™

No part of this book may be reproduced in any form or by any electronic or mechanical means, including information storage and retrieval systems, without written permission from the author, except for the use of brief quotations in a book review.

For my Mom, who had me in church from the day I was brought home from the hospital, and who tolerated my billion difficult questions about God and the Bible while I grew up.

I came that they may have life, and have *it* abundantly.

— JOHN 10:10 (NASB)

INTRODUCTION

Let's get something out of the way right from the start. Death ain't pretty. It's not pleasant. No one likes to talk about it. Fewer like to even think about it. But just like going to the restroom or having that weird dream of going to school on the first day of class in nothing but your underwear...it's something we're all going to have to face at some point or another.

So make no mistake. The book you now hold in your hands is about death. There will be times you might find me callous. Might be times you feel I'm flippant. But rest assured, as a forensic death investigator with more than twenty-five years' experience in the field, I'm awfully protective of my clientele. Protective of their families and loved ones. And while I might share a story or two of the more humorous aspects of my job, there is nothing but tremendous respect for those whose deaths I've investigated.

There will be some chapters that might gross you out. It'll be odiferous. It'll turn your stomach. It'll cascade down your mind's eye with fluids meant never to exist outside the body.

Truth be told, no matter how long someone has been doing my job, there's always another case in the future that will surprise them with the gross-out factor.

The cold hard fact of the matter is that death is an ugly thing. We try to sugarcoat it. Give it a Hollywood makeover. Dab a little powder on its nose, throw a little lipstick on it, and try to look past that ugly hair-flecked mole on its chin. But death is ugly.

Something most funeral directors or pastors won't tell you? There's never a pleasant way to die. It's always ugly. Foul. There's no dignity in it. Ever.

You see, death is a most unnatural thing. It was never intended to be part of our lives. As you'll see in the next chapter, there is a 'wrongness' to a corpse that's difficult to describe, but it's there nonetheless.

That's because God created us to live, not die. He created us to blossom, not wither away. He designed us to shine with His glorious light, not fade away into the shadows. But it happened. One day, in the world's first garden, a woman decided to disobey God. Her husband, not wanting to be outdone, followed suit. The first Sin. And with it, the universe began to decay. Light began to dim. Flowers started to wilt. And humans were introduced to death.

Death is unnatural. It's part of the Curse. It's part of the Fall of Man. It was never meant to touch us. And yet it does. And there's nothing we can do about it. So each of us lives our lives, one day at a time, hoping to keep the big black cloaked goon with the scythe at arm's reach for as long as we can.

But while we wait, there are some things that death can teach us. Lessons that can be learned by the tales of the dead. They might be repulsive to some, but the living should take heed, nonetheless. I guess the task of chronicling these lessons has fallen on me. I was the big dummy who chose to listen to what they had to say to begin with. I hope you'll follow along for the journey. It might be uncomfortable in some places, but I promise you...it'll be well worth the trip.

A Quick Word Before We Proceed...

Over the years, I've had many strange cases. Cases that would never make it into television shows like *CSI* for the simple fact that they weren't murders. They weren't whodunnits. They weren't glamorous or twisted enough. I've often said that, most often, the best cases to work in this job have nothing to do with crime. Nothing to do with murder or violence. There have been many sad cases. Just as many funny ones, if you can pardon my insensitivity in the matter. (In my job, one finds humor anywhere they can in order to survive.)

However, as I proceed to share some of these stories and impart to you the lessons I've taken from them, I want you to know that I have an obligation, as I've mentioned earlier, to the people who come through my office doors, and their families. I might have a sense of humor about some of them, but I always take the pain these families have endured very seriously, and treat their dead loved ones with the utmost respect.

Because of that, I'm somewhat 'fictionalizing' these accounts. Yes, I'm changing names and places. But I'm also tweaking a few details here and there in an attempt to save someone from the indignity of seeing their loved one's folly displayed for the world to see. The deaths and how these people died are very real. Nothing about the actual lethal circumstances have been altered. But hopefully enough of the settings, times, places, and people have been changed that it will be difficult to identify by anyone in the know. I owe it to these people to at least do that much.

But I feel these stories are important to share. I believe God can do great things with these tales of sorrow, strangeness and, yes, humor at times, and I feel I'm the most qualified person to share them with you. During our journey, there may be times you might want to stop and get off due to some of the content. I hope you'll stick around for the rest of the ride because I believe these lessons can change your life... or at least give you a little different perspective on the life you currently have.

So are you ready? Well, come on. Let me tell you about the time...

1
HER SOUL'S NOT HERE

It was sometime in the Fall of 1992 when I first stepped foot in a medical examiner autopsy suite. The fluorescent lighting hummed overhead, revealing the mold and mildew dotting the cracked floor tiles and unrecognizable stains on the metal walls. Though the employees there denied it was possible, my eyes burned with the chemical stench of Formalin and something even more pungent permeating the office space. Despite all this, my twenty-two-year-old self was near-bursting with excitement.

I was working on my bachelor's degree in Criminal Justice. The professor in my Introduction to Criminal Justice class assigned us each a special project: choose a criminal justice-related institution and spend the day, observe exactly what they do, and report back to the rest of the class when it was over.

My dream, of course, was to become a homicide detective. It's all I really ever wanted to do since squeezing past the astronaut/baseball/superhero phase of my childhood. Truth was, however, I didn't care much for the 'cop' stuff. I wasn't interested in wearing the uniform or driving fast down the street with the red and blue lights strobing stars in people's vision. All I wanted to do was solve murders. Crack the elaborate puzzles. Use my wits and observational skills to deduce 'whodunit'.

So when it came time for me to complete this special one-day field experience at a criminal justice facility, where do you think the best place would be for me to go? Most people wouldn't have ever answered with the city morgue, but that's precisely what I did. I figured the first, and more important step, in cracking the big case was with the autopsy, and that's precisely why I chose it.

When I got there, I was instantly overwhelmed by the sights and sounds. Keep in mind, back in those days in the Jacksonville Medical Examiner's Office, the front door was nowhere near the autopsy suite. Nowhere close to the bodies. Nowhere within viewing or smelling distance of any of the gross stuff that one might imagine goes on at such a place.

The office was old and crumbling. It had endured decades of the worst humanity had to throw at it. And, like people, buildings tend to start smelling funny the older they get. That smell—it's impossible to describe after all these years—was the first thing I noticed. I sat there, my legs shaking in the Naugahyde-upholstered waiting room chair, anticipating what was about to happen next. A few minutes later, an attractive young woman opened the door to the waiting area and greeted me. She introduced herself as an investigator at the office and told me that I would be shadowing her throughout the day.

I was so excited.

Having had my own eager shadows enough times over the years, I now know I should have pitied her. At the time, however, I had no idea. I had no notion of what to expect. No preconceived ideas of much of anything, really. There was no such thing as C.S.I. back then, so autopsies and morgues were kind of a mystery themselves.

The biggest whopper of a thing that I didn't know, however, was that the day would change my life forever.

Skip ahead a few hours. The place was bustling. People from all walks of life, moving through the cramped hallways, doing their day to day jobs. When I arrived, there had been no bodies—a rarity seldom seen by the same office today. I had little to do or see. So, the pretty young investigator began talking to me about what she did for a living. It sounded amazing. I was enraptured. I soon discovered that the medical examiner wasn't so much concerned with 'whodunit' as much as 'how it was done'. And when I considered what she told me, I realized something. I realized that that the 'how' was infinitely more intriguing than the 'who'. In a world where the majority of murders were committed by drug dealers versus drug buyers or husbands killing their spouses, finding the killer suddenly no longer seemed all that exciting to me. I'd much rather be part of the other side of the forensic spectrum that worked to figure out how someone died.

It wasn't until a few hours into my day that I managed to see my first dead body. She had been an alcoholic. She'd simply died in the bedroom of her home. Being poor she had no insurance, and therefore had no doctor capable of signing her death certificate. Because of that the medical examiner's office took jurisdiction, and she was wheeled into the intake area by two other investigators working in the office that day.

Wrapped tight in clear plastic, she was pulled out of the livery van on a stretcher. With a quick jerk of the arms, the woman was then pulled over onto a long metal tray that rested on four wheels. The tray was maneuvered over to the facility's scales, and she was weighed, measured from toe to top of the head, and log-in paperwork completed before she was shoved through the walk-in cooler doors and manhandled out the other side into the autopsy suite.

I followed her, still uncertain of what to expect. Then the autopsy technician began unwrapping the plastic sheeting, and she became more and more visible to me with each passing moment. A couple of minutes later, she was fully exposed. She'd been found naked at home, and that was exactly how she was displayed on top of that cold metal table. Her legs were discolored by bruises along the ankles and shins—telltale signs of the heavy drinker who bumps into furniture regularly as they stumble through their house. But there were no other signs of injury that I could see.

She reeked of urine and feces, but there was another odor as well. A pungent stench that burned my eyes even more than the urine. It was the smell of alcohol that had passed through the body's bloodstream, relieved itself of its intoxicating properties, and was simply left to saturate the deceased woman's veins.

But here's the thing. I honestly didn't notice. Once seen, the bruises disappeared from my mind. I quickly forgot about the smells. I didn't hear the doctor as she spoke to the investigator or the technician to prepare for the autopsy. I wasn't aware of sounds or smells, or the air conditioning on my skin. I was only able to focus on one thing at that moment —the weird five-foot-three-inch mottled purple and gray thing now lying on that autopsy tray that had been a human only hours earlier.

I was mesmerized by the sight, but didn't look at her in

the way I would eventually come to do quite naturally during the course of my career. There was no scrutiny for forensic details. No search for scars, marks, or tattoos that might identify her. No determining whether rigor or lividity was present. No careful hunt for track marks on her arms or between her toes. Instead, I was taken in by the body as a whole and the sudden absolute realization of the unthinkable: this is not natural.

There was a...wrongness to it. To this day it's difficult to put into words, except to say that it seemed unnatural to me. Perverse. Blasphemous even.

The woman, quite simply, was not a human anymore. As terrible and inhumane as it might sound, as I stared at her goose-pimpled flesh I found nothing about her resembling anything remotely considered a person. She had a head, two arms, two legs, a torso, and a head full of tangled hair, but for all intents and purposes she was—and I shudder to use this term for fear it makes me sound cold and horrible—a piece of meat on a slab.

As I looked at this now-dead woman, I had one thought and one thought only: *There is no soul here.* It's strange to admit, but it's true. It's one hundred percent true. Every word of it. Amid this amazing opportunity few people going into criminal justice get to experience—a real forensic autopsy—the only thing I could think of was that it was brazenly apparent that the human-like skin-sack of tissue, bones, and cartilage was distinctly different from every other person in that room. It was so obvious, like a bright neon sign pointing down at her, shouting in bold bright letters: "No Soul Here!"

I often say if you laid two people on the ground, side by side—one living and one dead—I could tell in an instant which one was alive. There'd be no need to check for a pulse.

No need to watch to see which one's chest moved up and down as the living one took a breath. No need to check the skin for mottled patterns of livor mortis. The assessment would be instant. And it would be accurate nearly every time.

From the moment I saw that very first dead body to the ten thousandth time, there are two things abundantly clear to me. First, there is such thing as a soul. Second, the moment we die that soul goes away.

And it's not just me. I've been working as a forensic death investigator for a long time now. During that time, I've been in the place of that first young investigator I met on that day a number of times. I've given tours and overseen internships more times than I can remember, and time and again I hear the same thing: there's something different about them. Something missing. It's as plain as day to anyone who takes time to pay attention. The living have souls. The dead do not.

So what does this mean? Why is this important?

Simple. If souls exist, and if they leave the body at the moment of death, where do they go? Many who believe in such things say that souls are made of energy. Energy, as science tells us, can be neither created nor destroyed. So, the soul must go somewhere, right? To the Christian, the answer to this question is obvious. If we have a soul, it will live on after our bodies turn to dust. The real question then is, where will our souls live on after that?

An Unnatural Tomb

There's no soul here.

The phrase I kept repeating over and over while I looked

at that poor woman on the autopsy table reminded me of another, similar phrase I'd heard before. Some women scurrying nervously up to an old tomb. An unnatural tomb in every way. A borrowed tomb. A tomb that shouldn't have been occupied at all. The women are on their way to prepare the body. A body of a man who should have never died.

Of all the deaths the world has ever seen, no death is as unnatural of that of Jesus. The 'wrongness' of Jesus' death literally shook the earth and made the sun hide behind a black veil of mourning. It should never have happened. Those bright eyes should never have dimmed. That quick smile should never have faded. That skin, tanned and leathered under the heat of a Galilean sun, should never have been torn, flayed, and skewered by a Roman's lance. But it happened. The Creator of all life had died. It's just indescribably wrong.

Those women crept up to that unnatural tomb, probably fearing discovery by followers of the Sanhedrin or the Romans, only to find its covering stone rolled away and lying flat on the ground.

"Why do you seek the living among the dead?" a voice asked them.

They turned to see an angel standing there. A brief exchange went on between them, and the angel said, "He is not here. He has risen."

The soul is not here. Jesus is not here.

Two very similar statements. Two very different outcomes.

The 'wrongness' of Jesus' death was temporary. The Giver of Life had vanquished Death and had risen. He'd returned to what was purely natural: a Living Christ. A Living God. A Conqueror over the wrongness of death.

He set right what was once wrong.

This, my friends, was the very first life lesson I ever learned in the morgue. I mean, I believed we had a soul. I thought we did anyway. But it wasn't until I saw that poor alcoholic woman lying lifeless on that autopsy table that I had irrefutable proof—at least in my own mind—that it was so tangible. So obvious. So real.

I also learned that death, despite the platitudes often given during times of grief that 'death is a natural part of life', is anything but natural. It's not the way things should be. Thankfully, I knew we had a Redeemer who had turned Death up on its ear so that we may all have the promise of everlasting life.

Despite the tragedy of the woman's death, this revelation gave me great hope.

I've carried that hope with me ever since. Never doubted it again, in fact.

2

DEATH BY GOLDFISH

CASE # 05-0434
DECEDENT: REDACTED, Jeremy
Re: Accidental Death

The piercing wail of the beeper ripped me from my afternoon nap. It had been one of those days that are so infernally hot that it sucks the air straight from your lungs. I'd already had two cases that day, both of them smack dab in the middle of a mid-August sun blazing its fury onto the back of my neck. I'd needed sleep in the worst way, so I went home to catch a few winks. Of course, in my line of work, working forty-eight hours straight, sleep isn't something you're ever promised.

"This is Holloway with the Medical Examiner's Office," I said to the Sheriff's Office dispatcher who answered the phone. "You paged?"

"Just a second," the abrasive voice on the other end barked before placing me on hold. Another three minutes later I was patched-in to the detective on scene, who gave me a brief rundown on the case for which I'd been called.

It seemed a seventeen-year-old kid, along with five of his buddies, had been out fishing in one of those high-end speed boats out on the river. There'd been some sort of accident, and the major crimes detectives were requesting me to respond to the local boat dock.

Great. More of that wonderful Florida sunshine, I thought, sliding into my Crown Victoria and firing up the engine.

Ten minutes later, I walked onto the wooden boardwalk overlooking the fresh water beach. Detective Bob Jensen, smiling from ear to ear, ambled towards me, the wooden planks straining under his massive weight. His grin threatened to split his face in two. It was a look that boded trouble for me. I didn't like it one bit.

"You are not going to believe this one," he said, shaking my hand with a laugh. "It's crazy."

"So what have we got?" I asked, walking toward the end of the pier and a slip berthing several boats of all shapes and sizes.

"I'll let you see for yourself."

It's never a good thing when cops don't immediately start going into debrief mode when I get to a scene. It usually means something exceptionally gruesome or weird. I can't say I was looking forward to discovering the surprise waiting for me.

The two of us made our way to a souped-up speed boat. Meandering deputies, along with a handful of crime scene technicians, shuffled out of the way as we approached. Once at the stern, I saw the victim lying lifeless inside. He looked so young. But then they always did when you've done this for as long as me.

The victim was face up, clothed in a pair of swim trunks, a tank top, and flip flops. His long, thick blond mane fell back to the floor of the boat like a big yellow puddle, and he sported a neatly cropped goatee with no mustache.

I climbed into the boat and crouched down for a better look.

"I don't see any signs of trauma," I said, looking up at the detective. "No rigor. Lividity hasn't even set in yet." Which only meant the guy hadn't been dead long. Something I already knew from my conversation over the phone.

The boy's face caught my eye. It was a dark purple. Oxygen deprivation?

"I don't see any froth around his nose or mouth," I said, referring to the typical white foam present in many drowning deaths. I paused when something odd caught my eye, then leaned in for a better look. "There's a bulge around his throat, though."

"Bingo," Jensen said with a smile. "He didn't drown, if that's what you're thinking."

"Bob, just tell me what happened. You know I hate these games of yours. I'm not Sherlock Holmes."

"All right, all right. Seems our victim here, and his pals, were out having a good time on their boat. Catching some rays. Doing a little fishing. And drinking. Lots and lots of drinking," he said. "Apparently this guy is a huge fan of *Jackass*."

"*Jackass*?" I asked.

"Geeze, Kent, don't you ever watch television?"

"Only the Syfy Channel and British comedies." I smiled.

"*Jackass*." The detective let out a sigh. "Johnny Knoxville? Little midget guy running around in diapers? Stupid guys doing stupid things?"

"Heard of Knoxville. He's the guy who's going to screw up the upcoming *Dukes of Hazzard* movie, right?"

"Yeah, that's him."

"I've never seen the show, though."

"You really need to get in this millennium, you know that?" he said. "Anyway, these guys on this show do all kinds of crazy stunts. They even made two movies."

"Let me guess. This guy decided he'd like to be the next Johnny Knoxville."

"Pretty much." Jensen shook his head as he lumbered down into the boat and knelt near the body. His chubby finger pointed to the victim's throat. "Knoxville's crew had this one stunt where they apparently swallowed a goldfish whole. And alive."

"So this guy died from swallowing a goldfish?"

"Nah. He thought he'd do one better." He stood up, his legs creaking under his weight as he wobbled to a cooler a few feet from the body. He opened the lid, letting me peer inside to see several varieties of fish on ice. "These guys were fishing, remember? Well, one of them caught a brim."

"Oh, for crying out loud. Don't tell me he swallowed it."

"He tried to anyway. The way I figure it, once swallowed the fish does what a fish will do. Dorsal fins probably expanded, then it got caught in his throat." Bob's face darkened at the words. "Poor kid didn't have a chance. His friends hightailed it to the docks as soon as they could. Even dialed 911 enroute, but they just weren't fast enough. Rescue pronounced him on arrival."

I glanced back to the kid lying lifeless in the boat. How many of these had I seen over the years? How many kids imitating their favorite shows...the world around them...had ended up in the cooler of my office?

My transport crew's arrival cut the thoughts away like a scalpel blade. I helped them bag the body, loaded him into the van, and headed back to the office to write my report.

The drive there wasn't pleasant, filled with thoughts of the world and visions of the calamities its system spawned.

Goldfish Crackers and a Dark and Dangerous World

Do you have kids? If not, have you ever watched brain-frazzled parents dealing bravely with their children in a park, movie theater, or mall? Then chances are you know something about Goldfish crackers. You know, those little cheesy bits of fish-shaped heaven that all kids seem to love. Usually, they're divvied out in clear plastic baggies like crack rocks to toddlers looking for a junk food fix.

The amazing thing is, they work wonders. They seem to calm kids down instantly. Ease the beast of boundless energy burning within them. Make them placid. Serene. It's as if the science of calorie physics is turned inside out or something.

And it all has to do with their shape. They look like cute little goldfish. To a four-year-old, the gross-out factor of eating a real goldfish is just too much to pass up. Sure, they're cheesily good, but then so are plain old, every day, square Cheez-Its. They're the same. Same color. Same taste. They just don't have the same effect. It's the goldfish that has the power. Or rather, their shape has.

Goldfish snacks aren't real fish that swim aimlessly in circles in a tiny bowl on the countertop until they're flushed down the toilet. They aren't the cute, aquatic versions of Chihuahuas for our children's amusement. They are merely a perfect blend of enriched wheat flour, cheddar, and Thiamin Mononitrate molded into the semblance of a goldfish.

They're imitations.

What's more, they offer little to no real nutritional value. According to the label, one 0.5 ounce packet of Goldfish crackers has 60 calories, 2.5 grams of fat, 120 mg of sodium, and 20 g of carbohydrates. They have plenty of calories and carbs for extra fuel, a ton of salt, but hardly anything of any real substance. As a matter of fact, if you really examine them, you'll find that they're made of mostly air. A thin cheesy crust with an air-filled center.

That's the way most imitations are. They're hollow. Valueless. They offer nothing truly beneficial to us in the slightest. Sometimes, imitation can prove downright deadly. As the young man in the case above discovered.

He'd been so captivated with a popular television show and the antics of the cast, he'd wanted to impress his friends by being like them. Even more, he wanted to show the *Jackass* guys up—out-do them. Instead of a goldfish, he decided to swallow a bigger fish.

A brim.

In case you're not an avid fishermen or a marine biologist, you should know that brim, or bluegill, have spiny dorsal fins that expand when excited. They're a defense mechanism. The moment our guy gulped down the fish it expanded, lodging itself in his throat. He suffocated.

I'm not writing this to bash the old MTV show or those like them. I'm writing this to reveal a truth. A very important, undeniable truth.

Ready for it? Okay, here it is.

It's been said that imitation is the greatest form of flattery. I say you'd better be careful who you're wanting to flatter.

You see, the world is a very dangerous place. It's full of panic, peril, and pain. It's laden with hurdles. Mined with folly. Super-charged with danger like a downed power line. And predators lie in wait for us to make one minuscule slip before they pounce.

Imitation Station

Despite the dangers lurking in the shadows of the world, it sure has its share of bright, shiny baubles, distractions, and pleasures of all kinds. Fast cars. Expensive clothing. High profile parties. And torrid sexual encounters. Celebrities, sports personalities, and the who's who of the rich and famous lavish themselves with endless streams of these hedonistic delights. What's more, they love shining the spotlight on themselves as they partake.

And they look so good doing it.

We eat it up. We buy supermarket tabloids. Watch trashy gossip shows on TV. Gobble up any and every bit of scandal surrounding our favorite celebrities we can find. Many of us begin desiring to be part of it all. We crane our necks at the picture window of celebrity and pant helplessly, like children looking at the new toy store display being erected for the world to see. And we want it. Badly.

But it's not just about the celebrities. It's also our neighbors, friends, and family.

Our friend down the street gets himself a brand-new Audi R8 convertible, and boy does he look good behind the wheel. Your next-door neighbor gets herself invited to their community's party of the year, and you're stuck at home, wiping your four kids' runny noses. Your co-worker is having an affair with the cute girl in accounting, and their rendezvous are so fool proof there's just no way in the world they'll ever get caught.

And you find yourself thinking, "Wow. Why can't I be like that?" Or, maybe, "It's not fair. I deserve to have that."

The world tells us we should have those things. The world says it's okay to revel in the pleasures it offers. It's only reasonable that you'd want a luxury car. It's not natural for a man to be faithful to only one woman for the rest of his life.

We don't just have needs, we have desires. And we need to placate those desires by whatever means we can.

What's more, the world goes on to tell us that all we have to do is imitate those we admire. Want to look cool like the Marlboro Man? Smoke some cigarettes. Want to be as funny as any comedian? Season your words with plenty of F-bombs. Want to feel sexy and beautiful? Have a surgeon sculpt your body into a playmate with implants and Botox. Simplistic examples, I know. Doesn't make them any less real.

The world tells you to play copycat to get the things you want. Do what we do. Talk the way we talk. Buy the same clothes and gadgets we buy. Eat at the same restaurants. Do the same diet. Do all this stuff and more, and you'll be able to live the life we live.

Doesn't sound so bad, does it?

So we begin imitating what we see. We act out the intangible fantasy world in hopes of catching one vaporous moment of happiness. But just like with those little Goldfish crackers, when we've taken a bite out of the "good life", we find it completely hollow inside. There's nothing of substance. Nothing to fill that void we're desperately struggling to satisfy.

And all too often we realize the truth only after it's too late. When we are gasping for breath, struggling to dislodge the spiny fins of despair crammed down our throats.

We finally got that sweet-looking convertible, but are drowning in bills to pay for it. We're finally invited to that party we've desperately wanted from the moment we moved into the neighborhood, only to be pulled over on the way home, and now face a DUI charge.

Oh, and that cute girl in accounting you've been eyeing? You finally get up the nerve. Think of the best way to approach an affair without your wife finding out, and have the time of your life. Then, a month later, in the middle of the night, you get a phone call. She tells you she's pregnant and wants to know what you're going to do to take care of her and the baby.

It all looks fantastic on the surface. It smells of success and prestige. We want to dive into the world feet first and just wallow in its pleasures. We want to soak up the intoxicating aroma of ecstasy.

Only, it's devoid of any substance. That kind of joy is as elusive and ethereal as a puff of smoke in a tornado. And when the wind shifts, we find ourselves completely alone to deal with the harsh reality of our actions. We've chosen to imitate the wrong thing. We've mimicked something that seeks one thing and one thing only—to smother the very life from our bodies and destroy us.

Why on earth would we want to emulate that? Is there an alternative? Is there something better to imitate? Is there something of truer substance?

You bet there is.

Be Imitators of Christ

All this talk about goldfish gets me thinking about the early Christians and the use of a fish pictogram to symbolize Christ. What is the parallel? Why did they use something so strange as a fish to represent the incarnate God of the Universe? Well, it has to do with the Greek word for fish. The English translation is *ichthus*. The first-century Christians used this word as an anagram to teach a bold theology and the backbone of their faith. The message?

In Greek, the word was *'Ichthys'*. The anagram used was *'Iēsous Christos, Theou Yios, Sōtēr.'* Or "Jesus Christ. God's Son. Savior."

That was what any believer would immediately think of when they saw the fish symbol scrawled out on a Roman wall. That was the message of hope the early Christians endeavored to spread throughout the world—that God's Son, the Christ, was Jesus of Nazareth, and that He alone was the Savior of all mankind.

And it is this very same Jesus, God's Son, Christ, and Savior that we should strive to imitate on a daily basis. He's the only one who will never lead us astray. The only one who will lead us from destruction and towards true, unadulterated joy.

How can I say this with confidence?

I'm confident because I've discovered that it's all about purpose. You see, it was never that brim's purpose to be swallowed whole and alive like that. It was never Jeremy's purpose to swallow it. Both of them were involved in an act outside God's purpose for their lives, in the pursuit of discovering joy.

The same can be said for the guy who desperately wants

that great automobile or the lady who craves to be part of the social elite of her community. Countless individuals seek out the missing joy of their lives in meaningless, and all too often disastrous, sexual escapades.

But whether we want to admit it or not, such things are simply not our purpose in life. They're not what God put us on the earth for. They have nothing to do with finding that special something that each of us earnestly seeks.

True joy never comes outside of our purpose. It is only found when we are fulfilling what God has planned for us from before the foundations of the world.

So what is our purpose? To imitate Christ. To grow more and more into the image of God's Son until the Day of Glory when we will all be perfected! That is God's purpose and plan for our lives. That is what each and every one of us is searching for...the meaning we long to discover.

In Philippians 2, Paul tells the church that they should "Have this attitude in yourselves which was also in Christ Jesus..." He goes on to describe Christ's attitude as one of humility. As one of servitude. As one of obedience to God the Father. And what does the Christian gain from doing this? The same as Christ, really. The opportunity to be blessed by doing God's will on earth. The reward of being raised up to do amazing things. The honor of serving the Creator of all that is. There is no greater reward than this. Believe me.

In many ways God did create human beings to be mimics, imitators, and impersonators.

When the Apostle Paul wrote to the Christians in Ephesus, he told them, "...be imitators of God, as beloved children..." Paul knew the same thing we do. A child learns by imitating his parent. He talks the way his dad speaks. He learns to toddle by watching his mom. And as he grows up, he begins to resemble each parent more and more. Likewise, the more we imitate walking in Jesus' footsteps, the more and more like Him we'll eventually become.

We are imitators through and through. We can't help ourselves. It's innate in our very souls. The trick is in discovering the object best suited to be imitated. And the answer to that is always Jesus Christ. He will never let you down. He will never lead you wrong. You will never, ever wake up one morning wishing you'd made a different choice.

For He alone is our purpose. He alone is capable of bringing us the joy we desperately crave.

Imitate the Fish, not the world that seeks to swallow it whole.

3

RISE!

CASE # 12-0116
DECEDENT: REDACTED, Loretta
Re: Probable Drug Overdose

I drove up the dirt driveway of a two-story residence overlooking the St. Johns River one Sunday afternoon, pulled up to the nearest police cruiser, and got out of the car. The place was nice. Lots of trees, varying from large oaks with their thick, finger-like branches stretching down to the ground and covered by hanging Spanish moss to a variety of palmettos and palm trees gracing the landscape with tropical beauty. Lots of shade. Lots of gnats swarming my head the moment I stepped out into the muggy heat.

And lots of people. All standing outside near their cars. Their arms crossed. Their heads bowed. Silent as the grave. They were in mourning. I recognized it instantly. A few sniffs. A few wipes of tears from their cheeks. No dramatic displays of anguish. But a family in pain nonetheless.

After grabbing a pair of gloves, my camera, and a

notebook, I walked up the brick walkway to the front door and gave it a gentle tap. A moment later Detective Steve Garner opened it, looked past my shoulder at the grieving family, and nodded me inside. Once I was out of view, he smiled and gave me a quick handshake.

"She's in the bathroom," he said, leading me through the house. "She and her husband woke up this morning. Had some breakfast. Then she just disappeared for a while."

Detective Garner went on to tell me of her long history of prescription drug abuse. It had started with an accident resulting in a back injury. Doctors, wanting to ease her suffering, lavished her with strong painkillers. It used to be a rather common story before legislators wised up to the problem. After a while, a tolerance for the medications develops, and they find themselves needing more...or stronger pills. That's what happened to our victim that morning. She soon found herself addicted to them. She'd hoard them. Take them whenever the mood struck her. Then go to the doctor with complaints of more pain to get another fix.

That morning, after breakfast, that fix killed her. The prescription bottle had been left out on the countertop in the bathroom. She was on the tile floor, halfway on a rug, face down. A small amount of vomit oozed from her lips onto the floor.

I snapped my photos, rolled her onto her back, and took more photographs. Then I examined her from head to toe, looking for signs of abuse, trauma, or anything suspicious that might explain her death other than the obvious. There were none.

With a sigh, I stood to my full height and turned to the uniformed deputy standing at the bathroom door. "Okay, let my guys in," I said, referring to the contracted livery team the county used for transporting bodies to our office.

"Um," the deputy responded, shifting nervously from one foot to the other.

"What's wrong?" Garner asked him.

"It's the family," he said. "Er, they'd like to see the body before you take her. Want their pastor to pray over her, if that's okay."

I always dreaded this request. On the one hand, I want to be sensitive to a family's needs during such a hard time. On the other hand, I have a responsibility to the deceased to maintain proper evidentiary integrity. A bunch of people standing around or touching the dead person could potentially leave artifacts that could mess up a case.

Then there's the unspoken issue with letting family members view their loved ones at a scene. It's something of an X-factor. An unknown variable. It's better known as emotions, and the problem with it at a crime scene is that it's unpredictable. Most of the time, the family will be very respectful and appreciative of the gesture of letting them say their goodbyes. Then there are the others—like the father who threw me against the wall as I tried to carry his baby out of his house.

This time, however, we had plenty of deputies on hand to maintain control, and there was nothing suspicious observed at the scene. I saw no reason not to grant their request, but I instructed the deputies to stay close by in case things got out of hand.

A few minutes later, my transport crew had the body on their stretcher, partially bagged and covered. Her head was visible and that was it. I did what I could to wipe the vomit from her mouth and nose, then they wheeled her out into the living room. A deputy motioned for the husband, a handful of other family members, and their pastor to come and say their goodbyes.

The deputies, detectives, transport crew and I stepped back, out of the way. We lowered our heads out of respect and waited.

The pastor eased up to the stretcher, placing a callused hand on the dead woman's shoulders and another on the shoulder of her husband. He began to pray. It was like any other prayer I had heard a thousand times before. Praise for the Father, who gave us life. Praise to the Son, who redeemed us. Praise for the Holy Spirit, who comforted us in times of grief.

Then, suddenly, I couldn't understand a word that was coming out of the pastor's mouth.

For a moment, I wondered if I'd had a stroke!

Then, it hit me. He was speaking in tongues. Over a matter of minutes, the strange language increased in both volume and cadence. The pastor grew more and more excited as he prayed. The more excited he got the more excited the husband and family got as well, and they began joining in the tongue-speaking prayer.

Detective Garner and I gave each other a sideways glance. I was a believer. An ordained minister, in fact. I respected these people's method of reaching out to God in Heaven, even if I didn't understand it theologically. It was just rather strange to me.

I had no idea what Garner thought of the whole thing. I wasn't going to ask either.

But if I thought things were weird before, I hadn't seen anything yet. Suddenly I heard a single word. Understood that word, too, though it left me scratching my head for a millisecond before understanding slammed me in the gut like a baseball bat swung by Babe Ruth.

"Rise!" the pastor had said.

"Rise!" the family repeated.

I blinked.

"Rise!"

"Rise!"

All hands were now firmly placed on the body.

The pastor's voice was even louder now. "Rise!"

The family's voices matched his, decibel for decibel. "Rise!"

I looked over at the detective and whispered, "If she sits up on that stretcher, there's going to be a Kent-shaped hole in that door behind us."

He chuckled, and we all stood there in nervous silence for several more minutes. But when she didn't sit up after a while, I knew it was time to bring things to a close. I walked over to the pastor, placed my hand on his shoulders, and in a quiet whisper told him it was time to wrap it up. Graciously he nodded, and after a few more minutes my guys were loading that poor woman into their van. She was leaving home for the very last time, but I prayed at that moment, with a family of such staunch believers, they would be reunited one day soon in their new Heavenly home.

Raising the Dead

Want to freak out a Southern Baptist? Start speaking in tongues within listening distance of them. They'll run for the hills like nobody's business.

Want to freak out *anybody in the world*? Start trying to raise someone from the dead.

We Baptists like to keep everything nice and orderly. The supernatural, we admit, is real, but we'd just as soon not have much to do with it if at all possible. Supernatural things are messy. They make for an untidy doctrine. Difficult to grab hold of and understand. So, it's best to just sweep a lot of things under the rug and pretend the Bible doesn't really discuss them. It's not that the Baptist denies the doctrine of speaking in tongues. It's just that they don't quite understand —nobody really does, by the way—the doctrine at all, and therefore it's just best to focus on the things we *can* understand.

So imagine that same Baptist, who was uncomfortable around something as innocuous as 'speaking in the tongues', now has to stand in the same room with a group of people who are trying to actually resurrect the dead.

Needless to say, I wasn't kidding when I told the detective I'd be barreling through the front door if the woman sat up. In my world, the dead had better stay dead. It'd just make me a whole lot more comfortable in my job if they did.

But I've got news for me—and you, too! The dead won't stay dead forever. There will be a day when the dead will awaken. A day when God knits the tissue and skin back together on skeletons. A day when ashes will burst from their urns, their molecules will bond together again, and the cremated remains will walk the earth again in a fully regenerated body. The dead will walk this earth again one day, completely renewed. One-legged amputees will once again have two legs. Organ donors after death will have their organs back. Like Lazarus walking out of his tomb, they will not be decomposed or mummified or anything resembling something dead.

No. There is coming a day when the dead will no longer stay dead.

That's the day all believers are waiting for. The day we're counting the ticks of the clock over. It'll be the greatest day we will ever know on this earth. The day the living and the dead in Christ will rise to meet their Lord face to face.

What an amazing day that will be. Of course, for nonbelievers, they might have a different phrase for it—a George Romero picture, maybe? But that's a lesson for another time. For now, let's focus on the miracle of the dead being made alive again.

Walking Zombies

As a Christian I always get rather annoyed, if not downright angry, around Easter time when the memes start pouring in on social media, joking about 'Zombie Jesus'. The world sees our belief that Jesus rose from the dead as a joke. Something to be mocked. The only explanation for someone rising from the grave, in their minds, is that they must be a zombie. Or a vampire. To them, the very notion of infinite God coming down and confining himself in the frail, fragile package of a newborn baby is preposterous. The idea of Him growing up, going to work as a meager carpenter, and living a normal life for his first thirty years of residency on earth is a little more believable. The Romans killing him on the cross? Equally as believable. After all, the man tried to get people to be nice to one another—a capital offense by the *powers that be* in almost any culture. Unbelievers easily recognize that fact.

But then they come to that one strange Sunday when everything in the universe changed. Peter described it as Jesus marching down into Hades and snatching the keys of death right out of the hands of the devil. Then He returned to his body, and walked out of the tomb as easily as you might walk out of a grocery store with automatic doors.

Jesus was dead. Then, He wasn't. He was unnaturally dead. Then He was naturally alive. The world just can't deal with it, so they make fun of the very idea and call him a zombie.

That gets me to thinking, though. Jesus' sacrifice and resurrection wasn't just so we will all be resurrected from the dead one day. That would be great all by itself, but God has a specific purpose for us while we're alive. Being alive in this world is important to His plan. So, Jesus wanted us to live the very best lives possible.

Jesus was also resurrected so we, as Christians, could live life to the fullest today. As He told His followers in the Gospel of John, "I have come that they may have life, and have it more abundantly."

Not just everlasting life, but a good life as well. The best life, in fact. A life filled with joy, even when we are sad. A life filled with purpose. A life filled with blessings of every kind. A life not dictated by our circumstances, but rather in our position as children of God.

As I write this, I wonder just how many Christians are out there not taking full advantage of this 'abundant life'. How many people have been restored to a spiritual life, only to walk around day to day as Christian zombies? Shambling their way through the living world in a daze, perpetual frowns on their moping faces. They have no direction; they just follow their feet wherever the wind blows, and hope something will come along to brighten their day.

This, for the Christian, is just as unnatural as physical death. Don't get me wrong. Jesus never promised us a happy life. Despite proponents of the prosperity gospel, He never promised us a wealthy life. He never promised we'd have no problems in this world or that we wouldn't suffer. Indeed, He told us we'd suffer more than most if we followed Him. We still live in a fallen, cursed world, after all. Why should we skim by with less hardship than the Christ we serve?

No, He didn't promise us happiness, wealth, or even security. What He did promise was an abundant life.

So what exactly does that mean? How can we ensure we're not living a zombie life—only partially raised from the spiritual dead and wandering the earth aimlessly without any joy, hope, or love? Where's some of that 'abundant life' you kept hearing about when you placed your faith in Jesus? Why did it disappear and how do you get it back?

It's About Attitude

I've just had a conversation with a co-worker, Kelly, who has an office right beside mine. Neither one of us are fans of the bright fluorescent lights shining down over our heads. It hurt our eyes. Gave us headaches. So, we both recently bought table lamps to give us soft, warm light that wraps around us like a two-thousand-thread-count cotton sheet. Mine just came in the mail today, is shaped like a human skull, and is way cooler than hers. I set it up, turned it on, and powered down the Death Star lights overhead. My tension melted away like an ice cream cone on a hot sidewalk.

When Kelly walked by my office afterwards, she told me it was now too dark in my office. She walked over to the window behind me, and proceeded to twist the blinds open a fraction of an inch or two. I protested, shooing her from my office so I could bask in the dimness that I prefer. We laughed about it. Talked about it. I demanded she never try anything of the sort again if she knew what's best for her.

It's all playful banter. We have that kind of relationship. But that's when she proceeded to tell me something that totally made my heart sink.

She told me about how much I've been complaining recently. She was half-joking, but I could tell she was a bit serious, too. Knowing me as she does, Kelly understood it was something I needed to hear. Something, down deep, I would want to hear, so I could correct my course and try to be better.

Plus, she just likes correcting me when I act like a jerk, but that's a whole other thing. Point is, I needed correction regarding my complaining and she was happy to give it.

See, there's nothing that saps the joy from our lives and inhibits an abundant life more than a complaining heart. Complaints are like stones being laid across the ground. Each complaint builds off of an earlier complaint's foundation, and a wall begins to form over time. The more complaints, the higher the wall, until one day you find yourself unable to see any of the blessings around you because you've imprisoned herself in a dungeon cell of gripes and grumbling.

If you can't see the blessings, you can't experience them. If you can't experience blessings, you can have no joy...no abundant life. No life to the fullest. Not the life Christ has planned for you. Complaints, you see, are connected to one of the greatest sin attitudes humanity has ever faced.

Pride.

It's probably the root cause of all sin. It's certainly the cause of the first sin. But a spirit of complaining stems from pride. It comes from the idea that our irritations and frustrations supersede everything else around us. It is an attitude of self-absorption. A worldview of being more important than anyone else we come into contact with.

Friends, an attitude like this strangles the joy from our lives. If we're always dwelling inward, we can never care about things outside of us. If we're always absorbed in our wants and our needs, we can never enjoy the things we have...the blessings that have been lavished on us by the Almighty God. It blinds us to the fact that joy and abundant life has nothing to do with our circumstances, because we're scrutinizing each situation under a microscope. Focusing on the problem, and not the problem-solver.

Don't live your life as a Christian zombie. I say to you today, "Rise! Rise! Rise!" Cast aside your worries and complaints, and enjoy the life Christ intended for you today.

4

MUMMY AND ME

CASE # 08-0098
DECEDENT: REDACTED, Margaret
Re: Unattended Death

Gail and her elderly mother, Margaret, practically beamed as they slid into their car and pulled out onto the interstate near Austin, Texas for their much-needed Walt Disney World vacation. The trip, which their GPS was telling them would take over sixteen hours in order to traverse eleven thousand miles of road, would be grueling, but it would give this mother/daughter duo a great chance to bond.

So, they slid a Glenn Miller Band CD into the car stereo, veered onto the interstate, and started making their way east. Along the way, they chatted it up. Margaret had become concerned about her daughter over the past few months. She hadn't quite been acting herself, but she couldn't quite figure out what the problem was. She just seemed more flighty than usual. More distracted. Occasionally she could swear her daughter was talking to people who weren't there, but she couldn't be sure. Granted, Gail always hushed such concerns away, stating Margaret was just being overly worried.

Maybe I am, she thought, glancing over at her daughter, whose hands were dutifully on the ten and two position on the steering wheel. *She's a good girl. If something was wrong, she'd tell me.*

So the two continued their way east. At one point, they decided it would be neat to make a detour—they weren't on any kind of schedule after all—to the nation's oldest city, St. Augustine. They'd heard wonderful things about it. Cobblestone streets that made one feel as though they'd traveled into the past. A beautiful bay in which one might still imagine pirate ships sneaking past lookouts in the dead of night. The Fountain of Youth! That sure would be something, wouldn't it?

Yes, after some discussion, the two decided a stop in the city founded by Ponce De Leon sounded like a perfect idea. The decision made them even more excited to put the miles behind them and get to the Sunshine State as soon as possible.

After a while Margaret slipped off to sleep, leaving Gail to navigate the traffic-heavy highway by herself. Everything was fine at first, but then nighttime came and Gail's eyelids began to grow heavy.

"Mom, I think I'm going to find us a hotel, okay?"

Not waiting for an answer, the daughter took the next exit ramp she came across, found the nearest motel, and paid for the night. The bed was comfortable and the air-conditioning thermostat was the closest thing to perfection Gail had ever experienced in her life. A perfect blend of temperature. Not too hot. Not too cold. Not like the car's air-conditioner, which had decided to go *kaput* on mile ninety-seven of their trek. The drive since then had been brutally hot, even with all four windows of the 1988 station wagon rolled down.

So for now Gail was just excited to have a little relief from the ridiculously high temperatures, and enjoyed the nice cool motel room.

It was the best night of sleep she'd had in weeks.

When morning came, Gail found herself perfectly rested and ready to tackle the rest of the trip after grabbing a quick bite at a local McDonald's drive-thru.

"Mom, you want anything?" she asked.

Ordering a couple of sausage biscuits, hash browns, a medium Coke, and a senior citizen coffee, the food was scarfed down quickly while sitting in the parking lot. When finished, the wrappers and empty cups simply tossed to the side with barely a thought, they quickly made it out onto the road again.

They stopped often, taking in as many of the sights as they could along their journey. Before reaching New Orleans, they made a quick detour to a few small towns along the coast, soaking in the sights, sounds, and boiled crawfish along the way. They stopped at flea markets they spotted along I-10. Their sixteen-hour trip quickly stretched into twenty-four. Then thirty-six. Then even longer. But they didn't mind. They were having the time of their lives.

The journey, as Margaret had always said, was where the joy of travel was truly found.

Gail began to think her mother had been right. They learned to eat while driving, stopping through drive-thru after drive-thru, chomping down on burgers and fries as they went, and tossing the trash onto the floorboards and seats of the car. It would be easy enough to clean up once they got to their destination. Right now, Gail didn't want to miss a second of fun with her mom.

The only thing she would have changed about their trip so far was their broken air-conditioning unit. Even with the windows rolled down, it was often difficult to even breathe with the oppressive wave of heat rushing in to greet them. But they made do. Margaret wasn't complaining about it, so why should Gail? Hopefully, they'd find some time once they got to Orlando to have it repaired before having to return home.

Soon they found themselves turning south on I-95, and traveled through the vast city called Jacksonville before moving into St. Johns County. Signs for St. Augustine's world-famous Alligator Farm and the first ever Ripley's Believe It or Not museum called to them like moths to a flame. Gail found her foot feeling like lead plates as she mashed down on the accelerator to get there faster. Her mother didn't seem to mind her excessive speeding either. At least, she didn't say a negative word about it anyway. Gail figured she was just as excited to be so close to their destination as she.

But as they neared the nine-mile marker from the exit ramp to State Road 16 that led into St. Augustine, there was a ding from a dashboard. A bright orange light warned her she was about to run out of gas.

Gail juggled the numbers in her head, calculating if she had enough fuel to get them to State Road 16. She thought she did, but one could never be too sure. As they passed the next exit she thought she might stop for gas there, but she saw no gas station signs anywhere.

Guess I'll just have to chance it.

"Don't worry, Mama," she said, slacking off on the accelerator to conserve fuel. "We'll be fine."

But if Margaret was concerned she showed no signs of it, and instead simply stared out onto the highway with great delight. A few minutes later, they pulled into a Gate gas station, and Gail got out to fill up the tank. When she was finished, she walked over to the passenger window and leaned in.

"I'm going to get us some drinks and snacks," she said. "Will you be okay out here?"

Without waiting for a reply Gail zig-zagged past a few cars, navigating the crowded parking lot of the gas station, and dashed inside.

If she'd turned around even for a split second, she would have seen the man standing at the pump opposite her car turn and stare hungrily at her mother. She would have watched as he tentatively took a step toward the car. Then another. His head turned left, then right, as if searching for anyone who might be watching him. Satisfied he was not observed, he moved closer still, scrutinizing the elderly woman inside the car. Margaret was oblivious to the man's approach. Helpless to stop him from doing what he was about to do.

Then he moved around to the passenger side of the car, looked inside the open window, and nearly fainted from what he discovered.

A few minutes later, the police arrived on scene. An hour or so after, the medical examiner investigator—my partner, Kenny—showed up.

"Where's the body?" he asked the lead detective as he looked the car over a couple of times.

Detective Jones nodded to the passenger side seat. Kenny drew closer. He had smelled the foul stench the moment he'd stepped out of his Crown Victoria. He'd been told it was the smell that had attracted the attention of the man who'd reported the death to the police. But as he approached the car, all he could see was a pile of trash stacked high in the passenger seat. McDonald's hamburger wrappers. Empty cups. Plastic bags. All of it piled into one big heap.

Then he saw it. The dark green marbled skin. Underneath the mound of refuse, Margaret's elderly body leaned back in her seat. She was decomposing. She'd bloated in some places. Skin began to sag in others. And in other places, like her arm and shoulder near the window where the hot wind had blown through, her skin was now black and leathery. Mummified from several days of traveling in a hot car.

Margaret, it turned out, died of natural causes soon after she and her daughter started on their trip. The daughter, who was mentally ill, had no idea. She continued on their journey as if nothing had happened, talking to her mother along the way as if she was still living. At the same time, for reasons never quite fully understood, Gail began the process of 'burying' her mother in the trash pile along the way.

Do We Have Blinders On?

Have you ever been accused of being oblivious? Having blinders on? So focused on your own world that you hardly noticed the orbits of others in your life? If so, you're not alone. It happens to the best of us. And yes, it happens to me all the time.

In fact, if there's one life lesson in this book that speaks loudest to me—heck, I'll say it...it pretty much shouts at me while beating me over the head with a big stick—it's this one. It's not that I'm insensitive. In a job that can easily make someone callous about the dead and their families, I'm often pulled in multiple directions by compassion for the grief-stricken loved ones and my need to do my job as impartially as I can. But all too often I become micro-focused on me. On my plans and goals. On my dreams. And as a rather avowed and contented hermit, on being left alone. When this happens, the blinders come on and I don't see anyone around me until they're slapping me upside my head to get my attention.

It's not that I don't care about them. Nothing could be further from the truth. I've been very blessed with a loving family, wonderful co-workers, and amazing friends. I care deeply about each and every one of them. But sometimes—all too often, I'm afraid to admit—my head slinks back into the hole of my turtle shell of tranquility and I put everyone else on hold.

I'm not sure if that was Gail's issue in this case or not. We did discover that she had serious mental illness issues, although the exact nature of her condition will remain confidential. On the one hand I believe, somewhere deep inside, she knew her mother was dead in the car. Why else would she try to cover her up with trash from fast food joints and convenience stores? There was a part of her psyche that must not have wanted to deal with the tragedy. On the other hand she told detectives she had no clue that her mother was dead, even though the elderly woman was partially mummified in the car, and the stench was nearly unbearable.

Was it denial? A good possibility. Was it mental illness? Most definitely. Could it have been something else? Let's just say it was all of the above and move on for now.

One thing we can say for sure, however, was that it wasn't malicious. It wasn't intentional. The daughter wasn't purposefully dumping her garbage on top of her decomposing mother out of lack of love or respect. It was just, quite simply, that the daughter was oblivious—for whatever reason—to her mother's current circumstances at the time.

It's an extreme example of being oblivious to the people around us, but it should be an eye-opener for us all. As a matter of fact, this case creeps into my crusty ol' noggin quite often whenever I become so introspective that I neglect the needs of those around me. Or at least I want it to, because as the poet John Donne so eloquently put it, 'No man is an island', and we all need each other to survive in this world.

Who's Riding in the Car with Us?

Now for the hard question. Who's riding in the car with us? When was the last time you checked the person in the passenger seat? When was the last time you looked to the backseat to see what's going on there?

Are they hurting? Are they in pain? Are they festering inside with worry and hopelessness? Putrefying with feelings of uselessness and sorrow? Are these passengers that travel with you day in and day out really dead inside, and you've never bothered to check?

It's easy to point the finger at Gail and accuse her of being unfeeling. Of being oblivious. After all, the signs of physical death are much easier to identify than that of an emotional or spiritual demise.

But that's precisely why we need to step out of ourselves

every once in a while. It's why we need to take stock of our passengers on a regular basis, like those school field trips when the teacher and bus driver made a roll call at every stop before pulling out. Make it a habit in your life, and I promise you won't regret it.

As I write this, I've just read a heartwarming news article about two eight-year-old boys and their first day of school. As one boy walks along the schoolyard, already nervous about the start of a brand new school year, he's overcome with sensory overload. All the other boys and girls laughing and screaming and running and playing as they make their way to class is just too much for him. He finds a quiet corner somewhere out of the way, hunkers down, and begins to cry.

A moment later, he feels a hand on his shoulder. Sniffing, the boy wipes away the tears and looks up into the smiling face of another boy. "It's okay," the newcomer says. "I'll walk you to class."

The first boy takes the other's hand and they begin strolling toward the double green doors of the school. They're both smiling now. They're both happy. They've both made a brand new best friend.

We can learn so much from children. I guess that's why Jesus was so fond of them, and insisted the disciples let them come nearer whenever there was a gathering of people to hear Him teach.

See, while children do tend to be selfish by nature, they have hearts big enough to focus on not only their needs but the needs of those around them, too. And they don't much care one way or another about differences in each other either. What I didn't tell you is that the first boy in this story has autism. The second boy is black, and in a predominantly white school. The black boy didn't care that the other was different. He saw a child in need, and he reached out in friendship. He didn't plan on changing the boy or making him better. He just wanted to be a friend. The autistic boy didn't see his new friend was black. All he saw was the smile on the other's face and the outstretched hand reaching down to him to pull him up.

Their differences were minuscule. Their newfound bond is a mountain of granite.

Friendship, man. It's where it's at. It's the stuff of miracles.

When we learn to step out in friendship...when we learn to look outside of ourselves and reach out our hands, miracles happen. Often, people aren't interested in solutions to the things that are plaguing their lives. They're just wanting someone by their side as they endure it. They just want someone in their lives who truly cares about them. They don't want to be someone's project. They don't want to be someone's 'ticket to Heaven'. They don't want to be someone's 'feel-good moment'.

They want a friend. And friendship means sacrifice.

The two greatest Christians I've personally known in my entire life are my youth minister and his wife, David and Donnie Garrett. The lessons they taught me while I was still a teenager have stuck with me to this very day. Both had hearts as huge and warm as the sun, but I think Donnie's heart outshone everyone's (I'm pretty sure David would agree).

Like many youth groups, we tended to sit together during the worship service. We all had our favorite spots. We all had our favorite people. We huddled around each other, slipping notes back and forth and enjoying the camaraderie. We'd all get swept up into our own little worlds.

Invariably, there'd be someone left out. Maybe they were the social outcast. Maybe they were new, visiting the church for the first, second, or even tenth time. Whoever they were, Donnie would notice. Whatever the situation, Donnie would take action.

How?

She'd assess the lonely teen and rifle through the mental roster of youth under her care, selecting the best match she could think of. A few minutes later, someone would feel that familiar gentle and loving tap on their shoulder, and feel Donnie lean in close to their ear from the pew behind them.

"He needs a friend," she would whisper. Or, "She needs someone right now."

And without question most of us would break out from our self-absorption, walk up courageously to that person we'd never met before, and invite them to sit with us. Normally, I would have been terrified to just go up to a complete stranger back then and invite them to join us. But with Donnie's loving words of encouragement, we were bolstered to move mountains.

Why?

Because I was once that lonely kid sitting in a pew by myself. My best friend had been that kid. Every one of us had been that kid. We all knew it. And we all knew that Donnie's heart just couldn't stand seeing a teen separated from their peers. She couldn't stand the thought of a single lonely kid. She despised outcasts—in that they were only outcasts because of apathy from others. Her heart was for the lonely. The downtrodden. The misunderstood. And she passed that heart on to each of us in the process.

So keep this in mind, every time you put your life in gear: check on your passengers. Make sure they're doing okay. Be there for them. You never know if doing so might just save someone's life.

5

DROWNING IN FILTH

CASE # 02-1285
DECEDENT: REDACTED, Robert
Re: Accidental Drowning

"Oh, my..." Dr. Leonard Moseley nearly choked as the black nylon body bag was unzipped. "That's absolutely the nastiest smell I've ever, well, you know."

I looked down at the dead man on the autopsy table, wrinkling my nose and trying to hold back the bile that was rising to my throat. Yeah, I did know. It was a gut-wrenching bad smell of the highest caliber, and threatened to make me throw up.

Don't ever let anyone tell you that a person in my line of work gets used to the odors, because if they do they're lying. Trust me, we get a whole lot of smells in the morgue. Decomposed bodies reeking of methane. Remains covered in maggots and other insects, which produce the even sharper smell of ammonia. Burned bodies, well, you get the idea. But this was a new one to me.

"And you said he was found at the bottom of a public latrine?" Dr. Moseley asked, as Matt, the autopsy technician, busied himself with photographing the body.

"Yeah," I said, walking over to the table and taking a closer look at the victim. He was literally covered in human waste, from head to toe. What was worse, it wasn't his. "Apparently, the guy gets his kicks out of watching women use the bathroom. He decided he wanted a better view."

"No way!" Matt nearly yelped. I could almost see his skin crawling up his arms at the thought. The funny thing about our autopsy tech—he spends all day with his elbows inside the torsos of our victims, yet was the biggest hypochondriac I'd ever seen. The guy is a germophobe to the highest degree! But since we'd hired him, the autopsy room had never been cleaner.

The photos of the body taken Matt hosed the victim down with water, washing away the filth that covered him. A normal-looking, business-type man revealed himself under all the muck.

"He's an accountant. Wife and three kids," I said to Doc as he gripped the scalpel and lacerated the man's chest with a typical "Y" incision. "Went to church every Sunday. Never been arrested. But he just had this fetish he apparently couldn't shake."

I watched stoically as the medical examiner pulled the skin of the chest back to reveal the ribcage. Matt handed him the tree branch loppers, which he used to cut open the ribcage.

"Go on," Moseley said, bending over the open chest cavity for a better look. "I'm listening."

"Anyway, like I was saying, he had this fetish. He liked to look at women using the bathroom. His wife knew about it, but she couldn't get him to break the habit. Detectives tell me his computer was filled with all kinds of porn showing the same kind of thing."

"Kent, just get to what happened at the campsite," Doc grunted as he pulled the spongy form of the victim's lungs from his chest.

"Okay, okay," I said with a scowl. Doc was all business. Only wanted to know the pertinent facts about the circumstances leading up to his death. "Our victim here goes to Nelson's Fish Camp, finds an unoccupied outhouse—"

"You mean a port-o-potty, right?" Matt asked as he pulled the bone saw from its drawer and plugged it into the socket.

"No, I mean a real, honest to goodness outhouse. It's a permanent structure built on top of a shaft twenty feet deep."

Matt's eyes grew to almost comical size.

"Yeah, I know. I couldn't believe it either." I grinned. "Anyway, our victim here goes into the outhouse, takes off his clothes, and ties off a rope near the base of the toilet seat. He then lowered himself down the shaft until he reached the bottom."

Doc busied himself at the dissection tray, cutting fine strips of muscle tissue away from the heart and putting them in a tub of formalin to be kept as evidence.

"So how long was he down there?" Moseley asked.

"No one knows for sure. He was last seen two days ago by his wife. Yesterday, someone noticed his clothes hidden in a garbage bag behind the seat. Then they found the rope."

The whirring roar of the bone saw erupted in the cinder block autopsy room, drowning out Doc's next question. I glanced over at Matt as he whipped the saw around the victim's cranium and popped the top off, revealing his brain. He flipped the switch and quiet thundered in the room again.

"I said, 'So how did he get stuck down there?'" Moseley repeated as he moved over the decedent's head and delivered the brain, placing it in a pan and weighing it.

"Oh, we're not really sure," I said. "It looks like, after getting enough, he tried to climb back up the rope, but it snapped somewhere halfway up. He fell about ten to twelve feet into the excrement. It took Fire-Rescue three hours to get him out of the hole, by the way."

"Well, it looks like he didn't die from the fall," Doc said, pulling his apron and latex gloves off and walking to the sink to wash up. "No cranial fractures. No bleeds."

"So what do you think the cause of death is?"

"I'm going to pend the case until tox comes back."

"Come on, Doc. Just tell me what you're thinking. I won't tell anyone."

He glanced over at Matt, who now busied himself with taking fingerprints of the body. "If I had to make a determination now, I'd say he drowned."

"Drowned? There wasn't any water in that—oh," I stopped when the realization struck me full in the gut at the implications. "Ah, gross, Doc! Are you sure?"

"Like I said, the cause of death is pending until I have a full toxicology report. However, from what I found in the lungs, I'd say our man here fell into the pit of excrement, inhaled, and sucked in an esophagus full of—"

"Poop?" Beads of sweat glistened off Matt's forehead as he moved towards us, his eyes nearly falling out of his widened sockets. "You've got to be kidding me!"

"I could be wrong. We won't know for sure until all the tests come back."

But he wouldn't be wrong. Doc Moseley rarely ever was, and we all knew it.

That's Just Nasty

The sewer. It doesn't bring to mind the most pleasant of thoughts. Most of us wrinkle our noses at the very mention of the word. I find myself even wondering about the look on your face as you read the case above.

Were you cringing? Were you tempted to turn to the next chapter? I wouldn't blame you.

But what you might not know is that there is a small percentage of people out there who have a fetish for human waste. They crave it. They revel in it. It fulfills a deep-rooted sexual urge that nothing else can.

I can't explain it. I don't understand why they're so drawn to it. All I know is the above case isn't the only one I've heard in my conversations with other medical examiner investigators. They're out there. Secretly basking in the worst humanity produces.

But I have news for you—we all do something similar. We all have the tendency to attach a rope to something in our lives and gradually lower ourselves into it. Slowly descending deeper and deeper into a muck we can't escape from. Eventually we try to pull ourselves out of it, only to find that the rope, our portal to the filth-free world, has been cut off or broken. We become trapped in it, and sink even deeper until we find that the filth is well over our heads, and we sink. The filth and mire pull us down, cutting off the air until we finally suffocate.

Can you guess what I'm talking about?
It's sin.

What's That Smell?

No matter how much we like to think otherwise, we all sin. Every single one of us, from the godliest to the downright ungodly. We are going to sin.

What's more, sin is the spiritual equivalent to human excrement. It is the byproduct of our fallen nature. It is secreted from out of us like a spiritual case of Montezuma's Revenge.

It's the reason sin disgusts God so much. It is nothing but filth to Him. Human waste. Take the gross-out factor that feces has for you and multiply that ten thousand times, and you kind of get the idea of how God feels about sin.

Yet, despite the fact that Christians are freed from the shackles of sin at the moment of our salvation, we gravitate right back to it like flies are drawn to a pile of feces.

We test it out. Place a toe in it. Then, we gradually lower ourselves into the mess like we would a hot tub and bask ourselves in the filth.

Don't believe me?

Then how do you explain the fact that so many Christians are secretly hooked on internet porn? Or what about pastors who run off with the church secretary? Do you know any Christians with addictions to alcohol or drugs? I bet you do, though you may not be aware of it.

What's more, we might be involved in these sins and not even realize it ourselves until it's too late. We just take a little peek on our computer screen one day and find ourselves up to our ears in it before we know it. We might take a little sip of a beer at the one party we go to a year and gradually slip into full-blown alcoholism in a few months.

Sin is like mire. It's quicksand. All we have to do is put one foot in and its vacuum sucks us deep inside it. The more we struggle the further we sink until, finally, we're just too exhausted to worry about it. We let it cover us. We try to breathe it in and we succumb.

But you might be saying, "I thought once I got saved, my sin problem would be over. What happened?" Well, let's talk about that for a few minutes.

Lingering Filth

Despite the fact that Christians are saved and cleansed of their sins, our primal nature to root around in sin like hogs in slop is still engrained in our DNA. Sin is a disease, inherited from our parents, grandparents, and so on. And even though we've been given the vaccination for it, we find ourselves having a tough time letting go.

Though our salvation washes us clean of the filth of sin, we might find that bits of sin still cling to us throughout our lives. Much the same way that the waste product still covered our victim even after being pulled out of the latrine.

These residual morsels of sin keep us from experiencing the full benefits of our relationship with God. They prevent us from gaining the abundant life that Christ said He'd come to bring.

And whether we want it to or not these pieces of sin pull

us away from our relationship with Him, towards more and more sin. It's an unending cycle.

So what are we to do? What can be done to stop it? The answer may surprise you.

We can't do a thing

The cold, hard fact of the matter is that we can't do anything to stop this from happening. There is nothing within our power to counteract the drive to drag us to the miry grime of sin. Like I said, it's innate in us.

That's the bad news. Ready for some good?

One of the most fantastic aspects of God's plan of salvation (besides the fact that He forgives us though we don't deserve it) is that He is continually working toward our perfection—to the day that we no longer sin. This portion of the plan is called sanctification.

Salvation is divided into three different stages. You can think of it like this: we were saved, we are being saved, and we will one day be saved. Let me explain.

Stage one is justification. Before this happens, there is nothing God will do in our lives. It is the moment in which He forgives us of all our sins and adopts us as His very own children. This is done completely by grace. There is nothing we do to earn it. Most importantly, it happens when we are still encased deep within the waste of sin. We're filthy, caked with spiritual excrement. And He reaches down His hand and pulls us out of it without a second thought.

Stage two is sanctification, and is what this chapter is all about. It is a process that begins at the moment of justification and concludes at the moment of the next stage. It is filled with ups and downs, spiritually skinned knees, and lots of bumps and bruises. It is where God takes the moments of our greatest weaknesses and most profound failures and patiently bends down and wipes away the mess, little by little.

Sanctification is where God painstakingly dabs away at those little chunks of sin still clutching onto us and throws them away, until all that is left is the third and final stage of salvation—glorification and perfection. Heaven.

So what? If we can't do anything to stop ourselves from sinning, should we just give in and trust God to take care of it all? As the Apostle Paul often said, "May it never be!"

While we do need to trust God to deal with the lingering remnants of our sin nature, we can't afford to sit idly by and let ourselves be swept away by our fallen natures. We must be vigilant!

One of the greatest failures of the modern church is its apathy towards teaching about the seriousness of sin. When I was in seminary, one of my professors would often beat a single fact into our heads: God takes sin seriously! So seriously, in fact, that He sacrificed His Son on the cross to deal with it.

If God takes it so seriously, and we are His children, how can we do anything less? That's why this chapter has been so graphic. It's why I've painted the most disgusting picture of sin I possibly could.

Would you willingly lower yourself into a pit of human feces? If you did, how much enjoyment would you get out of it? Not much, I'd venture to say. But sin is even more disgusting and dirty than any biological by-product! Its odor should tear into our souls, causing us to gag at the very aroma. We should grow ill at the very sight of it.

When we have developed a proper reference for sin in our lives, the struggle we have with it should become easier to deal with every day. If we see that computer screen with its pornographic images as a stained toilet bowl in an unkempt gas station bathroom, we might be less inclined to look. If we smell the vile stench of urine when we lift that bottle of vodka to our lips, we might be a bit more hesitant to take a swig.

So do yourself a favor: Don't lose the image I've tried to paint. Keep it close to you at all cost. It might just prevent you from climbing down that frayed rope into the mucky waste of sin.

6

THE FOUR-STAGE MAN

This next case doesn't have much of a story to tell. Just a dead guy in a house, who hadn't seen a doctor in years. No documented medical history. No physician to certify his death for the state.

It's the tale I hear pretty much all the time. Some out-of-state family members haven't been able to get a hold of a loved one in several days, and become concerned. They call the local sheriff's office or police department to go to the person's residence and perform what's called a 'well-being check'.

Nine times out of ten, the cops show up and no one answers their knocks at the door. They try to get permission from someone in charge of the property—property managers, lease owners or, in a crunch, the victim's family members—before forcing entry into the home. Sometimes they find a back door or a window around the side of the house unlocked, which makes it easier. Other times they're forced to take more drastic measures, such as shattering a window or busting down a door.

I don't remember exactly how the police got inside on this particular scene. It really doesn't matter. But after they did, and after they searched the house, they found him, naturally, in the last place they looked.

The bathroom.

The moment I walked in, I could tell it was strange. His position was unusual, hanging halfway on and halfway off the lip of the bathtub. His upper body, head, and arms were inside the tub. His lower half was draped on the outside. Where his shirt was stretched up away from his pants, I could tell he was beginning to mummify. The skin around his lower torso was yellowing in places as body fat began to slough away. He was wearing jeans, but no socks, and his feet appeared dried out and charcoal black.

I snapped a few pictures from my Polaroid (yes, this was before the advent of the digital camera), then leaned in for a better look. I blinked, scratched my head, and looked again. Inside the tub, his arms and hands were perfectly preserved. They looked as if the man was simply sleeping, and not in an advanced stage of decomposition.

I looked at his torso and feet again, then back to his arms and hands.

Weird.

That's when I saw his face. Or rather, his skull, picked clean and gleaming tan and white in the fiberglass tub.

I turned to face the detective, who shrugged. "We're kind of stumped about this, too," he said.

For a second, it was all kinds of confusing. One person showing signs of all major stages of decomposition simultaneously.

Before we proceed, I think it's important to share a little-known fact about television crime scene shows: they only have an hour to solve the crime, so in order to accomplish that they often fudge the science. Gasp! I know, right? Crazy. But it's true. As someone who's worked in this field as long as I have, I'm not a big fan of shows like *CSI* or *NCIS*, or any of the other alphabet soup shows. Mostly because they take themselves far too seriously. I always preferred the more comedic mystery shows like *Castle* or *Psych* or *Monk*.

Castle, as much as it pains me to admit this, was by far the worst to stretch the forensic science truth—especially when it came to pinpointing 'time of death' of their victim. They did this, of course, because the main plot point to the mystery always boiled down to a suspect's alibi. If you don't know when a person was killed, it's kind of difficult to catch the killer with a lack of an alibi. So, often, the two most common medical examiners on the show would confidently look over at Richard Castle and Kate Beckett, and announce, "He died sometime between 1:05 a.m. and 2:00 a.m. this morning."

Approximately a one-hour window. One hour for an alibi. One hour to solve the crime.

It's all hokum. I hate to say it, but that's not how it works. I can't tell you how many phone calls I get regularly from grieving family members wanting to know precisely when their loved one died. My answer is typically something like, "He died sometime between the last time he was seen alive and the time he was found."

I know that sounds flippant, but it's the truth. There's honestly no way to know for sure. There are far too many variables. What was his diet like? Did he drink alcohol before he died? Did he have a fever before he died? What was the room temperature? Did he take any medications? Was he covered in blankets? Was carbon monoxide involved in his death? These questions and more affect establishing a proper time of death.

The reason?

Because time of death—unless witnessed by someone, of course—is always determined by the state of decomposition. And, unfortunately, there's not a set rate and it's all dependent on so many factors that it's impossible to calculate.

There are general rules of thumb, of course. Typically, in the perfect environment (seventy degrees, minimal humidity, etc.), it takes about twelve to twenty-four hours for a body to go into full rigor mortis. It takes another twelve to twenty-four hours for it to come out of rigor. After that the body begins to decompose, and there are general rules of thumb for that, but they're so insignificant I won't detail them now. Basically, when a body begins to decompose, it gets more and more difficult to determine time of death.

So imagine my chagrin when I find this guy, showing all major categories of decomposition, lying in the bathtub. What was I to make of that? It's something I had never seen before, and it's something I've never seen since.

Of course, a little bit of deductive reasoning solved my dilemma. Many of you have already probably figured it out by now yourselves. It's just common sense, really. If you haven't figured it out, don't feel bad. I haven't given you all the information.

See, the bathroom had an electric space heater in it. The heater was turned on, and near the man's feet. The heater dried his feet out, causing the mummification. The heat dissipated slightly as his body drew away from the heater, so as it approached his torso the drying wasn't as quick or severe. That's why there was that yellowing skin around his waist. It was beginning to mummify, but it hadn't quite dried out completely. Of course, his hands and arms are simple enough. They were resting on the surface of the fiberglass bathtub. It was nice and cool there, which would naturally slow down the process.

See? Nice and simple. No real mystery at all.

What? The skull? Oh, yeah. That. Forgot to explain the skull. I was kind of hoping you'd forgotten that part, because this is where it gets kind of creepy. And a bit sad, if you're a dog lover like me.

Turned out, our victim had a little yapper dog. I don't recall its breed. Just that it was small and liked to bark. A lot. And his food bowl was completely empty when law enforcement arrived on scene. And...

Yeah, you get the picture. When it comes down to either starving or taking a nibble here and there on their dead owner, a dog is going to choose survival every time. And for some reason, animal predation most often begins around the facial area.

So poor little Fido survived, but at a cost of an open casket.

The question now is, how long had my victim been dead? Answer: sometime between the last time he was seen alive, and the time he was found. I'm telling you there's just no way to measure that with any kind of accuracy on the best of cases, despite what television tells you. Maybe one day reality will catch up to the fictional detectives we all know and love, but not quite yet.

Equal Parts of the Body

You ever awakened of a morning, or after a great nap, and discover your arm or hand is asleep? That strange pins and needles feeling of electricity zapping at your nerve endings? You try to pick up a pen or your glasses, and you struggle to get a good grip because the sensation is no longer there. You feel like your fingers have swelled up three sizes and everything you try to pick up seems as if it's covered in melted butter.

It's a strange sensation. Your brain is working fine. The rest of your body is ready to do whatever tasks need to be done. You feel full of energy, having gotten plenty of rest. And yet there's one part of your body that's giving you lip. One part of your body that's rebelling against your wishes. One part of your body that's now completely useless.

The only thing that can be done is to push through it and grab that pen anyway. Or wait for the circulation to return to normal. Either way, when a body part begins rebelling against us, it can be pretty annoying. Inconvenient. And, depending on what you're doing at the time, even dangerous.

In Paul's first letter to the Corinthians, he compares the Church to a human body with issues like this. In the twelfth chapter, while talking about spiritual gifts, he leans into an issue the church in Corinth must have been having with body parts completely falling asleep. Numb to the world around them. Useless.

He discusses how each gift (and gift user) is essential for overall health of the body. It's a passage meant to bolster those who feel shortchanged by their status within the body, and to humble the heady. It's designed to encourage the humble church greeter, librarian, or janitor, while warning the more visible church servants not to get a big head. He talks about how the eye can't say it's not part of the body or that it's better than the rest of the body. After all, what good would a body composed entirely of a single eye be? He says the same thing about an ear and foot. Each body part is important and essential to the proper functioning of a body. Take away a single part, and the body becomes unhealthy. Handicapped to a certain degree—like a finger that's fallen asleep trying to grasp a ball-point pen.

As I think about the above case—a body partially mummified, partially decomposed, and partially preserved—I can't help think, like Paul did, of the Church. After all, many local churches have the same symptoms, do they not?

How many churches have parts that are gangrenous? Putrid? Devoid of life?

How many churches have parts that are dusty and filled with cobwebs? Dry and crumbling?

And just how many churches have perfectly preserved parts that carry the load of the others, with a can-do spirit and determination to be flexible and serve the rest of the body, whatever their function?

There's an old rule of thumb among pastors and ministers. It's a concept ripped straight from the Pareto Principle, which essentially says that, in any given event, eighty percent of the results are due to twenty percent of the causes. In ministry, this has been turned around and rearranged a bit to say that, in a church, twenty percent of the people will do eighty percent of the work.

Does this resemble your church? Does your church have parts that have fallen asleep and become numb? Have they caused the rest of the church to fumble when trying to serve its mission? Are you one of those mummified dry feet or legs, causing the perfectly preserved hands to wither and dry up as well?

See, here's the thing about decomposition. It's caused by bacteria. Bacteria in the body, as well as bacteria in the environment. Leave a body in brackish water with well-balanced saline content for a day or two, and it won't decompose as quickly. That's because the salt halts much of the bacterial growth. Pull that body out of the water, and within hours—much faster than if the corpse had never been in the water to begin with—it will be green and bloating.

A body doesn't decompose all at once. It starts somewhere specific, then spreads. It usually starts in the abdominal area, then works its way out. The more bacteria there is to feed on the remains, the faster that decomposition occurs. So, with that analogy, the decomposed portions of any given church will quickly begin to affect the more preserved and functioning parts.

With a corpse, there's nothing you can really do about that. Fortunately, with a church, it doesn't have to be that way. Unfortunately, it all starts with you. The hand can't command the foot to take a step and the eye can't make the ear listen. What they can do, however, is fulfill their own purpose and let the brain (God) handle the other parts of the body.

So, here's what you should do: begin by asking yourself, am I perfectly preserved? Am I being useful? Am I fulfilling my purpose for the body? Or am I holding it back? Am I dried up? Withered? Am I bloated and blistering, sitting idly by while others do the work? Once you've established that, take the appropriate steps to change. It all begins with a change in attitude, by the way (remember that bit in chapter two about having the same attitude as that of Christ?). Yeah...

that's how it begins. Once you get that attitude readjustment, you'll find that pins and needles sensation fading away and you will once again be able to step out and fulfill your function in the body as you were intended.

Like I said, don't you worry about others. The brain will take care of them. If you're a hand—reaching out and helping people whenever possible—be the best hand you can be. If you're the feet—carrying the body along its journey so that God's plan can unfold—then walk without grumbling, and enjoy the trip. If you're the eyes—seeing where needs should be met—share your observations with the hands and feet. In the end, God is working to fine-tune us. Working to perfect us in a way that will make the church one mean, lean body to do His work on earth. We just have to let Him.

7

MARSHMALLOW SUITS AND CRIMSON

So not all my stories and anecdotes are full of decomposing bodies, blood, guts, and gruesomeness. There are plenty others that show the lighter side of my work. Silly stories of worker relationships and crazy antics that would make for a perfect sitcom. There's lots of humorous yarns dealing with the public or news media or funeral directors and doctors, in which no dead people or blood or guts even make an appearance. This next account, however, isn't one of them.

Well, that's not necessarily true. The blood and guts and stuff do make an appearance, but it's only in the periphery of a far lighter tale than I've told so far. It's also rather funny, and a bit embarrassing...for me, anyway. But it's one that begs to be told, and as a faithful chronicler of the dead that I am I have no choice but to tell it.

It's the story of an autopsy and the discomfort of wearing the horrid personal protection gear we use when eviscerating a body. You see, that gear basically consists of light blue plastic coverall aprons that cover your arms, shoulders, torso, and legs. You slip it on like you would a hospital gown and tie it off in the back. Then, you layer up with latex gloves, a mask, and a clear plastic visor to protect your face and eyes. Some people even slip booties over their shoes for extra protection. And while the autopsy room usually stays pretty cool, all that gear on is sweltering hot. By its nature it doesn't allow one's skin to breathe, so the heat accumulates and you sweat profusely.

Truth is, after performing a single autopsy in that get-up, I often feel as though I've begun to grow my own fungus farm under my clothing. It's miserable.

Fortunately, my job doesn't require me to assist in autopsies very often, but there have been plenty of times in the past where I've been required to due to staffing shortages, sick days, and just overwhelming case load. It's not my favorite thing to do on the job, but it's sometimes a necessary evil and I do it without complaint—most of the time.

Nowadays, we do autopsies a little differently. The doctors do most of the heavy lifting, and the forensic tech assists as the autopsy moves along. But years ago, in a time of a different doctor than the one I currently have, the one acting as a tech did most of the evisceration while the doctor sat back, enjoying a half a pack of cigarettes while he waited. On one particular Monday, our one and only tech had called in sick. I was the investigator on call, so it fell to me to pick up the scalpel.

Oh, how I dreaded it. Not the actual autopsy, mind you. That part can be backbreaking at times, but for the most part it's fascinating. No, what I dreaded was 'suiting up'. Putting that horrible, non-breathing, hot, sticky plastic on over my regular work clothes. Now *that* was truly unappealing to me.

But I've got one whopper of a fatal flaw in my duffle bag

of flaws. I've always fancied myself as more clever than I actually am. So, this time around I had an idea. I was going to get innovative. I was going to do something new and unusual. Something different that would make the experience a lot more bearable. Instead of that swamp-forming blue plastic apron, I decided to go for something a little lighter. A little more breathable. I decided I would slip on a 'marshmallow suit' and use that as my personal protection gear.

What's a marshmallow suit, you're probably asking? It's what I call a Tyvek suit. You know the ones. You see them all the time on *CSI* and *Forensic Files*. Those white zip-up coveralls with a hoodie and booties all those cool forensic kids are wearing. They're basically made of a paper-like material. Porous. Breathable. They're still pretty hot, but they tend to let the heat out much better than the plastic.

"Hold on there, Kent," you're saying. "Paper-like? Porous? You must be some sort of numbskull."

Here's me, nodding my head and pointing an index finger at my face.

If the material was porous, naturally it wouldn't exactly be a great way to protect oneself from, say, blood or other bodily fluids, right? Yep. Exactly. But, while I do tend to be a bit messy when performing an autopsy, I had always been pretty good at keeping the mess off my body while doing it. I just figured that the little bit of fluid that might splash up and hit me would be fine. It wouldn't be enough to soak through.

Well, my plan almost worked.

I had eviscerated and removed all the organs without hardly a drop of blood landing on me. I was pretty proud. And once again, I was much more comfortable so I was quite pleased with myself. The doctor finished up his part, dissecting each of the organs after weighing them and dropping a few specimens in formalin for testing later. When he wrapped it up, it was time to clean everything up.

And that's when I did it.

As I pulled the body from the autopsy table to the stretcher, blood pooling underneath him went flying. It splashed all over my stomach and waist in a great big splash. I instantly felt it soaking into the clothes I had on underneath.

Now, I don't typically cuss. I've never developed the habit, thankfully. But at that moment, I was sorely tempted. Biting my tongue, I finished cleaning up the autopsy suite, then turned my attention to the more immediate needs of cleaning me.

As you can imagine, our office comes complete with a pretty nice bathroom that has a good-sized walk-in shower. Having never had to use it, though, I hadn't come prepared. The only towels I had at my disposal were the hand towels we had on hand to clean the morgue. If that wasn't bad enough, I didn't have any spare clothes either. But I had blood all over me and I wasn't about to let it stay on me for long. I hopped into the shower, cleaned myself off—this might have included more rubbing alcohol and soap than was actually needed, by the way—then dried myself off as best I could with the tiny towels I had on hand.

I'd already tossed my blood-soaked trousers into the biohazard bin. I had nothing but a few minuscule hand towels to cover myself.

Thankfully, our office is comprised of two buildings: the administrative building and the autopsy suite. No one else was inside the suite but me. So I acted quickly. Dashing out of the bathroom, butt naked, I ran to the supply closet where we kept all our personal protection gear, and grabbed a new marshmallow Tyvek suit. I struggled into it—my still-wet body making the simple feat a most difficult task—and finally managed to zip it up to my neckline.

Finally, I was covered. I could now comfortably leave the office to go home and get a new set of clothes.

Yeah, did I mention still being wet when I slipped the marshmallow suit on? Remember when I said these suits are paper-like? I might have been wearing the suit, but I certainly wasn't covered. It was literally like one full-body wet t-shirt on me. There was no way I could leave the morgue like this. So I did the only thing I could think of.

I grabbed a set of those blue plastic aprons and slipped them on over the Tyvek, then slipped out the morgue door and into the outside breezeway that led to the parking lot.

But my humiliation wasn't over just yet. See, the administration building across the breezeway is lined with windows. Lots of windows. At the time, there were two female co-workers working in that building. At any given moment, a simple turn of the head and they would see me. And though I was now wearing the suffocating apron I'd wanted to avoid all along, it only covered my front. Not the back.

Yes, my still-wet rear was quite exposed for the world to see, and I had about fifty yards of open space before I could get into my car.

So, I pressed my back against the breezeway wall, and began shambling sideways toward the gate that would let me out and into the parking lot. I wasn't fast enough, though. A few steps to my left, and I saw two laughing faces in one of the windows. They had seen me, and were quite amused by my discomfort. Ignoring them I shimmied to my left, slipped through the gate, and ran as fast as possible to my car with a blushing ego.

The Best Laid Plans…

Ever heard the expression, 'If you want to make God laugh, tell Him your plans'? It's fairly accurate. Our best-laid plans often turn into disasters. We often think we're so clever. We think we've got this game called Life all figured out. We start believing we don't need His or anyone's help as we navigate our way through the day. We come up with smart schemes and life hacks, thinking we're pure geniuses, and BAM! A pool of crimson fluid is soaking right through those plans like water in a Bounty commercial.

As a result, we're humbled. If we're wise, we'll stay humbled. But not many of us are all that wise. It'll happen again. And again. And again.

The Israelites know this from throughout their history. Their hubris led them to wander a desert for forty years to get to the Land of Milk and Honey. The journey should have only taken them a few months. Their cleverness caused them to be subjected time and again to invasion and enslavement, until their eventual humility brought about a judge to deliver them. Their rebelliousness demanded a human king over a divine one. They received a line of kings who were buffoonish, if not downright despotic.

So tell God your plans. See what happens then.

Try, Try Again

I don't want to discourage you. But to continue with this lesson, I had to first put things in perspective. Our plans aren't always the best for us. Honestly, while I think God probably does have a pretty good sense of humor, I don't think He ever takes pleasure in our failures. He never laughs at our expense. But, like any good parents, there are times He needs to put us in our place.

So what are we supposed to do? Should we let our dreams drift by without trying? Should we give up any and all attempts at doing anything? After all, if it's not God's will it surely won't succeed. Right?

Often, when we fail at something—when that humility comes our way—we feel like failures. One too many failures lead to apathy, then eventually a desire to never try at all. Never take a risk again. Never reach out for that dream or attempt to love again, or whatever it is you've failed at in the past.

But that's not what this lesson is about. It's not about giving up. It's not about quitting. It's not about never trying.

It's one of teamwork.

See, I made a huge mistake that day in the autopsy suite, and it wasn't trying to be innovative. It wasn't experimenting with the personal protection gear (it wasn't the brightest move on my part, but it wasn't the real mistake either). No, the thing I did wrong was that I tried to fix it on my own. I was so embarrassed that I didn't want my coworkers to know what was going on. I tried to sneak out without their knowledge of the circumstances. I tried to get to my car without even seeing if there was anything they could do to help me out. Truth is, any one of the ladies in the administration building that day could have run to the nearest store and picked me up a pair of pants. But I was too prideful. I didn't want to endure the jokes and the laughter of my discomfort (you know how co-workers can be), so I tried to fix everything on my own. I failed miserably.

Lesson learned.

Here's the thing, though. God doesn't want us to quit. He doesn't want us to stop trying. He doesn't want us to put aside our creativity and cleverness for fear of failure. On the contrary, He created us in His own image. That means, like Him, we're creative geniuses. Like Him, we're always planning and building and inventing. Like Him, we're always pushing the boundaries of what is possible. He designed us this way. He wants us to be this way.

When God struck down Nimrod and his people with babbling tongues as they built a great tower to reach Heaven, it wasn't because the people were trying to get to God. No matter how tall they built that tower, it was never going to stretch to Heaven. No, when He confused their language to halt progress of the tower, it was to show them who's boss. It was to show them that they couldn't get to Him by their works alone. They couldn't reach Heaven by their own hands. Only He was powerful enough to bring humanity to Himself.

While that's an extreme example, it also works in our everyday lives. God wants us to try. Even more, He wants us to succeed. We are His children, after all. What parents want their children to be losers? No, He wants us to win. He wants us to thrive. He wants us to be successful in all we do. He also wants something else. He wants everything we do to be the best we can do, so that He can be glorified through it.

In 1 Corinthians 10:31, Paul said, "Whether, then, you eat or drink or whatever you do, do all to the glory of God"

(NASB). Everything we do should glorify Him. Because of that, we should put our best foot forward in all of our endeavors. He wants us to succeed, because our success, through Him, will be His success.

But we forget about the teamwork all too often. We forget to include Him in our plans. We think He's too busy for this little project of ours. 'I won't bother Him with this. I'll just handle it, then call on Him when it's something really big.' But that's not what He wants. Like a dad who wants to work with his son to build a Pinewood Derby car or a mother who wants to show her daughter how to make Grandma's world-famous peanut butter pie, God wants to spend time with us through our enterprises. No matter how great or small. He desires not only for us to succeed in the things we do, but He wants to be included in those projects as well.

And, most importantly, He wants us to listen to what He has to say about those things. We might think we know how to run that jigsaw well enough to craft the best Pinewood Derby car there's ever been, but God knows where the dangers lie. He knows what's been tried before. He's seen the track over and over again, and knows where the angles on that car should be. He wants to be our guiding hand through everything we do.

If we learn to do that, we'll be amazed at how successful we become.

Our Plans vs. Our Rebellions

There's one more thing I want to talk about before wrapping up this chapter. God doesn't just want to team up with us in our enterprises. It's important to realize that, more than that, He wants us to align our plans and our projects with His. It's not good enough just to ask God to help us out as we trailblaze a path outside of God's will.

Nimrod's tower wasn't being built just so the people could reach Heaven. They weren't just trying to get closer to God. They were building the tower in order to usurp God. They wanted to overcome Him. They planned on taking His throne. They not only were making plans without Him, but they were openly rebelling against Him as well.

Same with the prophet Jonah. God's plan was for Jonah to travel northeast by land to reach Nineveh. Jonah's plan was to travel southwest by sea to get as far away from that wretched city as he could. In the end, God's plan won out. It always does. And by the way, in God's plan, a 'goldfish' swallowed Jonah and he *didn't* die.

In everything we do, we must do all for the glory of God. Out best-laid plans will only succeed with God's approval, and along with His own will. When you busy yourself with an exciting new venture, never be afraid of failing. Nothing good ever comes by not trying. Not trying is the easiest thing in the world, and the results are always the same. Nothing. So give those dreams of yours a chance. Just be sure to seek God's counsel in it. Be sure to invite Him along. Ask Him to carry the heavy loads. And, most importantly, see to it that it aligns with God's wonderful vision for your life.

8

DEM OL' BONES

CASE # 95-1014
DECEDENT: REDACTED, Gladys
Re: Unattended Death

My partner pulled the Suburban up the long driveway, stopping just behind a patrol car before putting it into park. From the passenger's seat, I looked out the windshield. At least a half-dozen uniformed cops—all wearing fancy gold bars on their lapels, signifying the upper brass of the sheriff's office—milled around the unkempt front yard of the little cottage house in the Arlington area of Jacksonville.

"You ready?" my partner asked, looking over at me.

I call Investigator Jeff Brokaw my 'partner' but, in fact, he was training me. I'd only been working at the medical examiner's office a few months and was still getting acclimated to the work. This was going to be the very first skeletal remains I'd ever seen, so I was more than excited about it.

Dem Ol' Bones | 73

I nodded back to him, gathering the Polaroid camera, gloves, and a notebook, then slid from the cab. We both met at the front of the truck, and he proceeded to give me further instructions.

"I just want you to kind of watch me. Take photos where I tell you to," he said, glancing around the yard for a detective he could talk to about the case. "Try not to step on anything important. It shouldn't stink in there too much, but if you need to throw up try to get outside as fast as you can."

I'd already encountered my first decomposed body and had handled it like a champ, but anyone who does this job long enough knows that how well you handle one scene doesn't reflect how you might handle another. Everybody is different. Every scene has its own sights and sounds. And you never know if you happen to be fighting a bug of some kind that hasn't manifested until you come face to face with the worst death has to offer. He wasn't being mean or condescending by telling me that. He was simply being a good trainer.

Once again, I nodded my understanding. Then we started walking toward the law enforcement brass, hoping the lead detective would spot us and come to debrief us on the story.

We didn't have to wait long. Soon Detective Ramirez walked over to us, sweat glistening off his brow in the intense June heat. He dabbed his forehead with a handkerchief as he shook Jeff's hand and nodded at me. He then began to tell us the story of the little eighty-six-year-old lady whose remains were inside the house we'd just pulled up to.

Ms. Gladys lived alone in that house. While elderly, she had been spry enough that her family, who lived out of state, hadn't felt the need to place her in an assisted living facility. Instead, they paid the neighbor across the street to watch after her. The neighbor was to take her grocery shopping, handle her bills, take her to doctor's appointments, and anything else the old lady needed. And the neighbor had done her job beautifully for several years.

Then, five years earlier, the family had tried calling Gladys. Concerned when she didn't answer their phone calls they called the neighborly caretaker, who told them that their mother had taken her RV on a trip, and wasn't home yet. They seemed to pacify them for a time, but they'd eventually call back. When they did, the caretaker would offer another excuse for Gladys's inability to answer the phone. Eventually, over time the caretaker began telling the family that Gladys was angry with them and had no interest in speaking to them.

This went on for five whole years. Though hurt, the family wasn't suspicious because Gladys' social security checks were being cashed. Her banking was still being used. They assumed the old lady had plenty of money and had decided to use it while she still could. But after five years of this, they could take it no longer. They decided to take a trip to Jacksonville, to visit their elderly stepmother.

When they arrived at her house, they were greeted by a grisly sight.

"She's fully skeletonized," Detective Ramirez told us. "Lying on the floor of the living room."

He went on to tell us that it looked like the woman had died five years before, and the caretaker had known about it. But instead of reporting it, she had been taking the old woman's monthly checks and cashing them for herself. She was currently at the sheriff's office, being questioned by other detectives.

Amazed at the tale, Jeff and I followed the detective around to the back of the house, where the door was open. As we climbed the steps up to the back porch I noticed the door frame was cracked, as if forced open by a crowbar.

"Did you guys do that?" I asked, pointing to the damage to the frame. Often, law enforcement will have to force open a door to get inside a home, but I knew from his story that the family had entered the house using a key when they found her. I was confused by the damage.

The detective shook his head. "It was like that when the family found her," he said. "We think burglars broke in some time ago. Probably saw the body and hightailed it out of here before taking anything."

He led us inside, through the kitchen and hallway, and into a large living room. The air was stale and thick with dust. It was stuffy and humid and dark, despite the early afternoon daylight outside.

"The electricity was turned off years ago," Ramirez answered our unspoken question. "The caretaker saw no need to keep paying for utilities that our victim didn't need. It just meant more money for her own pocket."

The room itself was cluttered. Junk lay strewn on the floor throughout most of the room. In the center of the room was a clump of bedding—fleece comforter, piled with several blankets. It took a moment for my eyes to find her amid the folds of cloth, and only then after we flicked on our flashlights and came closer.

She was lying on her right side, her arms bent as if they'd been under her chin in sleep when she died. A mass of great black hair capped the brown-colored skull still resting on a pillow. A blanket was pulled up to her chest, covering the rest of her skeletal body. A can of Campbell's chicken broth, a hole punched in the top, sat half-empty next to the pillow on the floor.

I looked over at the detective.

"We think near the end, it was all she had to eat," he explained. "Looks like the broth was the only nourishment she had."

"You mean she drank it straight from the can? Not diluted with water or anything?" I asked.

"Looks like it. Yeah."

I sighed, then crouched down and snapped a few Polaroids of the body and its surroundings. After I finished, Jeff bent down and removed the blanket covering her. As the detective had already informed us, she was completely skeletonized. There was nothing left of her now, other than the bones and the hair on her head. There was no muscle, skin, or tissue of any kind. Just the bones. Just the hair.

And an old rat's nest within what had once been her chest cavity. Shredded piles of old newspaper and debris from the rest of the house lay in a circle among her fallen ribs, and I gasped at the sight.

"Haven't seen any signs of rats here," Ramirez told us. "They must be long gone by now."

But that wasn't my concern. It was the condition of the body itself that disturbed me on this scene. The depravity of her neighbor for letting this poor old woman waste away to nothing all these years. The gullibility of her family for believing the caretaker, and waiting five whole years to check on her well-being. I was angry. I was mortified. And there was nothing I could do at that moment but do my job and trust that justice would be done.

Abandoned and Alone

Ever feel like you're the only person in the world? Ever feel like no one knows what you're going through or that no one truly cares, even if they do? I think at one point or another, we all feel that way sometimes. For some people it's not just 'sometimes'. They feel this constantly. It's always somewhere lurking in the back (or forefront) of their minds. They feel as though everyone they've ever known or loved has abandoned them. They feel as though their entire life has been spent on a desert island, adrift from the rest of humanity. They feel as though, no matter how crowded the room may be, they are invisible, unwelcome, or unloved by everyone there.

In some instances this, unfortunately, might be very true. For others, it might merely be imagined. Tricks of the imagination. Symptoms of psychological distress. But despite the possibility that it isn't real, it doesn't make feeling this way any less painful.

At the end of our investigation, it fell to Investigator Brokaw and me to transport poor Gladys back to the office, and we had to do so while preserving the overall position of the bones as closely as possible to how we found them at the scene. This, of course, is no mean feat when there are no ligaments to hold the bones in place. It's not like those old Abbott and Costello movies. Skeletons don't miraculously stay fully assembled. Once the tendons and ligaments are gone, they fall apart. In order for us to keep the poor lady as much together as possible, we had to lift her up by the fleece (sheep-skin) bedding underneath her, and carefully place her in the body bag.

Sometimes, when we feel utterly alone and abandoned, it seems as though we might fall apart, too. Come apart at the seams. We feel disconnected from everyone around us. There's no support. Nothing to hold us together.

We need something to support us, like the bedding underneath Gladys. Something that will keep us together. Something that will preserve us as we're jostled on the journey of life. The question is, where can we find such support when we have no one to truly rely on?

Friends Forever

When we get down...when we feel utterly helpless and alone...when we feel as though we're unraveling, there's nothing worse than hearing empty platitudes. Having someone tell you, "It's just in your head" or "It's going to be okay. You're not alone," doesn't help the problem. It exacerbates it. It makes our feelings seem trite. Unimportant. And frivolous.

This only helps to strengthen the feelings of abandonment.

It's all well and good to offer verbal support for people who are suffering in this but, to use a cliché, action indeed speaks far louder than any words ever could. Unfortunately, people often get so caught up in themselves and their own lives (not to mention insecurities) that, although they mean well by telling you they're there for you, they fail to follow it up with anything more meaningful than a temporary ear with which to gripe. Often, they don't even lend that ear.

They simply tell you these things so they don't have to listen to your complaints any more.

The neighbor in the case above had promised to take care of Gladys. Had promised her family she'd look after her. Had promised the woman herself that she'd watch over her, and make sure she had everything she needed. And while, in the end, the caretaker hadn't intentionally killed her, she had failed miserably on following through on those promises. And a beautiful woman died and eventually disintegrated into bones and dust because of it.

But I've got news for you. Really good news. And it's no empty platitude. It's not a line of bull with nothing substantial to back it up. Jesus Christ will never abandon us. He will never leave us. And when He makes a promise, He always keeps it.

Don't believe me? Consider this.

Jesus' good friend Lazarus had died. He'd been buried and in the grave for about four days. They didn't have embalming back then, so as he lay in his tomb Lazarus began to decompose. His family was concerned that he would already be stinking when Jesus asked them to roll the stone away from his tomb. But that's the point I'm trying to make. After Lazarus had been dead and in the grave for several days, Jesus shows up to bring him back to life. He didn't give up on Lazarus. He didn't abandon him to his fate. Jesus' friendship is truly forever. Whether living or dead, Jesus remains steadfast and will never ever turn His back on us.

"Yeah," you might be saying. "But what if I do something bad against Him? What if I turn my back on Him? What if I deserve for Him to abandon me?"

Nope. He still won't give up on you.

The night Jesus was arrested and shuffled through Jerusalem to secret trial after secret trial, His right-hand man, Peter, was accused by rabble rousers of being His disciple. Peter. The big man with a short fuse. The guy who cut off a soldier's ear when he tried to arrest Jesus. And what did this disciple of disciples do when people asked him about his relationship with Jesus in the dead of night? He denied knowing Him. To emphasize to the crowd what he thought about Jesus, he even cursed. Now *that's* abandonment. Hardcore.

Fast-forward a few days. Jesus has been executed. He subsequently rose from the dead. Now Jesus could have easily just ascended into Heaven without so much as a word to anyone. Or He could have appeared to those disciples who had remained loyal and steadfast through it all. He could have even decided to start fresh and choose brand new disciples for His post-resurrection self. But that's not what He did. Instead, He met with His disciples in the upper room. He spoke with Peter on several occasions, even commissioning him to be a leader of His Church. As far as I know (the Bible is silent on this subject), Jesus never even rebuked Peter for denying his relationship with Him. He simply treated Peter the way He always had—with unconditional love and infinite patience.

Let that sink in for a moment. Peter denied Christ on the night He was arrested. In fact, he denied his relationship with Jesus three different times that night. He even cursed at the accusations. Now, to me, there's nothing worse than disloyalty in a friendship. I can admit I'd be hard-pressed to simply forgive and forget such an act by one of my friends.

But Jesus? Didn't even cross His mind not to accept Peter,

warts and all. Jesus doesn't give up on us. He doesn't hesitate to forgive. And He'll never abandon us.

And most of all, when we need Him most He'll always be that sheep-skin blanket we can lean against to hold us together when we feel like we're falling apart. That's a guarantee.

9

DEATH BY CURSE

CASE # 18-0236
DECEDENT: REDACTED, Gloria
Re: Undetermined

I pull up near the overcrowded parking lot of the beach's public pier and step out of my car. Despite the high winds the temperature is blazing, and sweat instantly starts soaking my shirt, pants, and socks as if I'd stepped into a shower. To the east, beyond the ocean's crisp blue horizon, dark foreboding clouds loom. Flashes of lightning cut their way through the clouds in the distance, signaling to us that our time at this scene is going to be very limited. A storm is coming, and it would be on top of us within the hour.

Detective Weis notices it, too, and jogs over to greet me. His eyes are fixed on the clouds, but I notice there's something else there, too. A look of concern? Worry?

"Thanks for getting here so quickly," he says to me, shaking my hand.

We start walking toward the entrance to the beach. He talks as I slip on my black latex gloves and pop open the lens cap to my camera.

"This is a weird one," he says.

So that's what seems to have him spooked. It's the case, not the weather.

"How so?" I ask.

I follow him to the wooden steps that lead down to the public beach, and we carefully begin descending.

"A jogger's dog got loose," he says. "Starts sniffing around the dunes. When the owner comes over to get him, she notices a bad odor."

We start making our way to the dunes to my right. Stalks of sea oats sway back and forth with the ocean breeze.

"Curious, she starts searching and finds our victim," Weis continues.

We navigate through the dunes until we come to the body. It's a young female. That much I can tell from a quick glance. She's on her knees, her face planted face down in the sand with her arms stretching forward, as if she'd been praying when she died. Although she is wearing a pair of shorts, she is completely topless.

And from the look of things, she'd been out here for a while. Her natural brown skin is even darker across her exposed back, which had literally been baked by the sun. There don't seem to be any injuries to her. Not that I can see from her backside, that is.

"We found a towel, her purse, several bubble wrappers of sleeping pills, and a half-drunk can of beer over there." Weis nods to our left, where a crime scene tech is busy taking photos.

"Sleeping pills?" I ask.

He nods. "Over the counter stuff. A few pills appear to be missing, but doesn't seem like a whole lot."

Carefully, I roll her onto her back. Her legs remain bent at the knees. Her arms are still outstretched from rigor mortis. But the rigor is dissipating. Her joints are already loosening.

Weis grimaces, shrinking back from the smell that erupts from moving her. The skin of her face and chest are marbling, already turning green in places. She's quickly decomposing, and the odor makes it evident even without looking at her.

"I'm guessing she's only been out here since early this morning," I say. "The heat and the alcohol would speed up the rigor."

I look her over. She looks like a thirty-something-year-old Hispanic female, if I had to guess. Nothing remarkable to note. No signs of injury. No signs of strangulation or anything suspicious, that I can see anyway.

"So what's got you so freaked out about this case?" I ask him. "I don't get it. Probably an overdose, if I had to guess."

He shrugs. "Ordinarily that would be my guess, too. But this one's got a bit of a backstory to her."

He has me intrigued.

He goes on to tell me her story. Apparently the woman lived in Jacksonville, Florida, and practiced Santeria, a common religion among Hispanics that has associations with the occult and other Caribbean religions like voodoo. Weis explained that a few weeks back, this woman had received word that her Santero, or priest, had placed a curse on her. But this was no ordinary, run of the mill curse, mind you. The working he'd performed was reportedly an 'Iku Brujeria'—literally, 'Death Spirit Black Magic'. A Death Curse.

Naturally, the young woman was concerned. She'd spent the better part of two weeks running frantically around town, searching for ways to beat the hex. But no matter where she turned, she could find no way out. She was going to die and there was nothing she could do about it, she had told family and friends.

"So, here she is," Weis says, gesturing at her half-baked, decomposing body. "No signs of trauma. No obvious cause of death. She's just here lying on the beach, dead. Like the curse finally caught up with her."

I blink at the detective, who stands about a head taller than me and is packed with muscle.

"Seriously?" I ask. "That's what you're going with? Death by curse?"

"Until the doc tells me something different, yes." He casts a sideways glance, as if searching for unseen eyes. "I spoke to the Santero before you got here. Dude admits to sending the curse. Even told me he'd put one on me if I didn't show him some respect, then reminded me there wasn't a jury on earth that would convict him for it either."

I shake my head with a laugh. "Well, duh. But have no fear, my friend. I think you're safe for now. And I don't think any curse killed our victim here, either."

He crosses his arms over his chest. "What makes you think that?"

"How many curses do you know that strip a woman of her shirt? Or drug her up with sleeping pills and beer? No, if I had to guess I'm pretty sure one of two things happened here, and neither have anything to do with black magic."

"Oh really, smart guy? Care to share?"

I grin back at him. I love a deductive challenge at a scene, and I'm ready to put my reasoning skills to the test.

"First possibility," I say, "I think our victim was so distraught she came out to the dunes to pray to God for deliverance from this death curse."

"But she's Santeria," Weis says. "Don't they have, like, a lot of gods?"

I shake my head. "Santeria, over the years, has been integrated into the Catholic Church's belief systems. Many of the spirits or gods they worship have been incorporated into the Catholic pantheon of saints." I pause, wiping a stream of sweat from my forehead. "So when dealing with a death curse brought on by black magic, who better to pray to than the Creator of everything...even the creator of the death spirit 'Iku'. My guess was that she took the pills and consumed the beer to ease her nerves as she prayed. Eventually, she got loopy. Drowsy even. The drugs, and the rising heat this morning, might have made her get extremely warm, necessitating the need to remove her shirt as she prayed. Eventually she passed out, and I think she probably died from exposure to the sun and heat."

He stares at me a few moments, as if he can't believe what he's just heard.

"Okay, wise guy. What's the second possibility?"

"Huh?"

"You said there were two possibilities. What's the second one?"

"Oh." To be honest, I hadn't even really considered the other as being remotely plausible. I'm betting my first guess was the most likely scenario. "Well, the other alternative is similar to the first. Only, instead of praying for deliverance, she just decided to beat the curse the only way she knew how."

Weis raises an eyebrow, waiting for me to continue.

"She intentionally overdosed on the sleeping pills and killed herself."

Death by Curse?

So, right off the bat, I'll be honest with you. I was totally wrong on the first guess. However, my second guess was correct. Ms. Gloria overdosed on the sleeping pills. She died from an overdose, and the amount of pills in her system was far too much to ever have been considered accidental. She would have had to intentionally ingest a huge number of pills to have what she had in her system.

She left no note, but notes are becoming increasingly rare these days.

But after interviewing her family and friends, it became clear. She was so distraught over this death curse that she intentionally invited the death curse into her life. She killed herself simply because she believed death was inevitable; she no longer wanted to postpone it.

Self-fulfilling Prophecy

Have you ever heard the term 'self-fulfilling prophecy'? It basically means that someone's belief in something causes the expected outcome to occur. Believe in a curse, and you'll face the wrath of that curse. Believe in a blessing, and you'll be blessed. Believe in ghosts, and...you guessed it...you'll see ghosts. Believe in unicorns? Well, okay...you probably won't see unicorns unless you're taking some really powerful medications. But you get the idea.

Belief. It's a powerful thing.

It can be wonderfully beneficial. It can be outright dangerous. It's also something that we should be careful of using willy-nilly.

One of my all-time favorite TV shows was the short-lived space western *Firefly*, created by Joss Whedon. The show only lasted one season, and culminated in a feature-length movie in theaters called *Serenity*. In the show, the crew of the spaceship Serenity is made up of a ragtag group of pirates and smugglers, a prostitute, a doctor and his sister, and a pastor. Now, this pastor never really talked about his beliefs specifically, but he did quote the Bible a few times. The captain of the ship, played by Nathan Fillion, didn't put much stock in religion, but he did develop a reluctant respect for the pastor during their time together.

In the movie, the pastor is inflicted with mortal wounds. He's dying in Nathan Fillion's arms. And as he dies, he pleads with Fillion's character to believe. "It doesn't matter what you believe," I'm paraphrasing what he said in the movie. "Just believe in something."

I was always disappointed with that line. To me, it's probably the single-most irresponsible line in movie history (and that's saying something!).

Why do you think I've got a problem with it? What makes it so irresponsible? Isn't having faith a good thing?

In short, no. It's not a good thing. Most of the time, belief and faith are outright disastrous. The reason for this is simple. Whether belief or faith is a good thing depends completely on the thing you believe or have faith in. People in Iceland still believe in elves. True story. A recent poll showed that about ninety percent of Icelanders still believe that elves, or the fae folk, are real. This belief is so strong that governmental policy dictates that if they're building a road, and come upon what is believed to be an elf habitat, they will actually build around that habitat. That's how pervasive their belief in elves is.

Do elves exist? Um, I think that's probably a topic for another book. Is it a bad thing if people believe in elves? Not overtly, no. But belief in such things at the cost of disbelief in the Truth most definitely can be bad.

Gloria's belief in Santeria, the power of her Santero and the spirits they revere, was bad for her. Her faith in her religion was so strong that she took her own life to avoid one of its consequences, which ultimately proved to be the consequence she was trying to avoid to begin with.

We must be careful in choosing what we put our faith in. We must be cautious when deciding on what to believe. This is why God has given us a standard for our beliefs through Scripture. It's why it's so important not to pick and choose what we like from the Bible and what we don't. It's why we can't afford to trust others to tell us what God's Word says, and why we should study it and learn it for ourselves. The Bible is the blueprint of all that is truth. It guides us, along with the help of the Holy Spirit, to discernment and understanding.

I grew up in the South. And I remember a few doctrines that were taught to me by my pastors, Sunday School teachers, and others that seemed strange to me even at an early age. For instance, I was taught that, although Scripture teaches 'once saved, always saved', if you commit suicide you're bound for Hell. The argument there was that it was the unpardonable sin because you die while committing a sin and are unable to ask God to forgive you for it.

As I matured, this 'doctrine' continued to bother me. It didn't make any sense to me. After all, if a person gets killed while robbing a liquor store, he dies while committing sin and has no time to ask God for forgiveness. But I never heard a preacher tell me that that was the unpardonable sin.

Then there's the fact that Christ's sacrifice on the cross was for all sin—past, present, and future. Once we're forgiven, we're forgiven for life. Not only had I been taught that suicide was a one-way ticket to Hell, but I was always told by the very same preachers that after I'm saved we ask forgiveness for our sins, not to maintain our salvation but to maintain our fellowship with God. In order to remain close to Him...in order to draw closer to Him...we need to deal with our ongoing sin. It's part of the sanctification process of salvation.

So, as an adult, these two incongruous teachings bothered me. I set out to discover for myself what was true. And guess what? Nowhere in Scripture is there even a hint of the false doctrine that suicide will instantly send a person to Hell. In fact, the Bible is quite clear on what the unpardonable sin is. Mark 3: 28-30 tells us that the 'unpardonable sin' is blasphemy of the witness of the Holy Spirit in regards to who Christ is. In other words, rejecting the truth that Christ Jesus is God and the Redeemer. And here's the beautiful part: it's not unforgivable at all until a person dies. Until a person dies there is every hope that they will receive the message of the Holy Spirit concerning

Christ, repent of their sins, and be reborn as a new creation.

The unpardonable sin is a sin that no true Christian can ever commit. Now *that's* great news!

But the point of all this is to remind us that we should be careful what we choose to believe. We should be cautious of teachers who share peculiar theological doctrines. We should question the things that we're taught, and study the one true standard of Truth all the time—the Bible—in order to know what is right and what is wrong.

But how do we know what's true in the Bible and what's not? I suppose this, too, is a matter of faith, but I personally believe the entire Bible is completely true and without error. People, whether preachers or theologians or politicians or celebrities, who try to decide what's true and what's not true in the Bible run the risk of playing a great big game of Jenga, with the blocks of their soul on the line. If one part of the Bible is wrong, it is impossible to know what parts of the Bible are correct. If you remove one portion of Scripture, it's impossible to know which portions of Scripture need to be removed next. So you might as well toss it out entirely.

In 2 Timothy 3:16-17, Paul writes to Timothy and tells him that '*all* Scripture is God-breathed' (emphasis mine). If God breathed life into it, how can any of it be wrong? If God brought Scripture into our world through the inspiration of the Holy Spirit in its writers, then how can we not be ensured that, throughout the centuries, He also inspired the Church fathers to choose the inspired books of the Bible and discard those that were not? If God breathed the Bible into existence with His own creative touch—just as He created us—how can we not trust that He would work to preserve Scripture through the centuries to remain pure and true?

Belief is a powerful thing. Belief has the power to heal. It also has the power to kill, as Gloria discovered. We need to choose what we believe very carefully. Our souls could depend on it. So what better place to seek what we should believe and not believe than in the Word of the Creator of the entire universe?

10

IF THE GLOVE FITS

CASE # 95-0108
DECEDENT: Unknown Male
Re: Undetermined

"Kent, can I see you in my office?"

I looked up from my desk, where I'd just plopped down after a long drive into work. My heart rate was drumming against my temples to beat the band. Whenever my boss, Bob Gastopulos, asked you into his office, it typically wasn't for anything good.

I glanced at the clock on my wall. I wasn't late. Got to work right on time. As far as I knew, I'd done everything right from my shift last night. I couldn't think of a single reason Bob would want to see me in such a formal manner.

I tried to swallow, but my throat was about as dry as an hour glass.

I stood up and shuffled into his office.

I'd only been working at the medical examiner's office for a few months. Still getting my bearings and learning everyone's personalities. I'd worked hard to get this job, and wasn't ready to get fired now. The look on Bob's face was dour. I must have really ticked him—or someone—off to get this kind of greeting this afternoon.

"You wanted to see me?"

He eyed me up and down, then nodded to the chair across his desk. "Take a seat."

Oh, Lord. I'm getting canned. I just know it.

I did as he instructed, then looked expectantly over at him. A few seconds later, he smiled.

"I'm sorry, man," he said. His grin widened. "I just can't do it to you. Your face is priceless."

I felt my heart leap into my dry scratchy throat. I was confused. "Do what to me, sir?"

He shook his head. "I was just messing with you. You're not in trouble. I just need you to do something for me."

A wave of relief washed over me, and I found myself breathing again. It felt good. But I was also a little ticked. Still, I wasn't fired, so I was quite happy.

"Sure. No problem."

"Oh, don't be so sure about that," Bob said. His smile was now stretching the laws of physics. He was certainly enjoying himself. "You're not going to like this." He paused, cocking his head to one side. "Or maybe you will. It's kind of cool if you can get past the grossness of it."

With that he stood, motioning for me to follow. He then led me through the office, out into the garage, and over to the autopsy building. When we entered the autopsy suite, there was a tray already pulled out and in the middle of the floor. A body inside a body bag sat on top of the tray.

"I need you to take fingerprints of that guy," he said,

pointing at the body bag. "Day shift couldn't get to it today, so I need you to do it."

I shrugged. "Like I said, no problem."

He chuckled. "You say that now. We'll see what you say when it's all said and done." And with that Bob strolled from the autopsy suite, leaving me alone with the body.

Interlude

Okay, before I continue there're a few things you need to know. Every so often, a medical examiner's office gets a body that's been dead for quite a while. People die wherever people are, and sometimes those places are pretty remote. Or closed off. Maybe the person who died has no family or friends. Maybe they're hermits, or live far out in the country. Whatever the reason, there are often people who aren't discovered for days, if not weeks, after they've passed away.

There is a pattern to most people's decomposition after they die. I thought now would be a good time to share with you some 'rules of thumb' regarding the time table in which bodies change.

Now, usually, given the 'perfect' environment (seventy-degree temperature, low humidity, no fever when they died, not lying under a vent or near a heater, etc.), it takes about twelve hours for a person to go into rigor mortis. Rigor usually lasts another twelve hours or so, and then the body begins to go flaccid again. After that, decomposition begins.

Usually decomposition begins in the abdominal region, where all the bacteria thrives within the digestive tract. As organs begin to break down, this bacteria is released and begins to eat away at more organs. Gases are released. The body begins to bloat and turn green. After a while, the green grows darker and darker. The skin begins to slough off the body, too.

And...you get the picture. No point in grossing you guys out any more than I have to in order to get my point across. The thing is, the body will continue to decay until, eventually, it's nothing but bones and strands of tissue and hair.

Lucky for us death investigators, most people are discovered before rigor mortis ever dissipates. But there are a few throughout any given year that are found right smack dab in the middle of that decomposition phase. That bloated, dark green mess of a body that is pocked with large blisters filled with methane gas. The slightest of touches will invariably pop those blisters, and the investigator is standing in a room with tears in their eyes from the intense smell.

Now keep in mind that every person who comes through our office has to be identified. Those fresh corpses still in rigor are usually pretty simple to identify. If your state has a governmental database of driver's licenses, then identification most often occurs through comparing the victim's face with that of the official government-issued photo ID. Other times, family members at scenes, who found the body generally, can offer a visual identification. [Side note: I can't speak for every state or every medical examiner's office, but I wanted to point out that all those cop shows on TV are usually wrong when they show family members going to the morgue to view their loved one in some drawer in a cold, clinical autopsy room. Although I do know of some jurisdictions that do that, typically that never happens. Identification is handled in a variety of different ways without having to disturb the family any more than they already are.]

Anyway, back to the topic at hand. Like I said, identification of a fresh corpse is pretty simple. But what happens when a body is decomposed? Bloated? Their skin is peeling off them? I'm not going to go into detail what this process does to a person's face, but it ain't pretty, and there's no way anyone can visually identify someone like that by a photo. So what can be done?

Well, there are a few scientific methods that might work for identification. Dental records are always good. But that only works if the deceased actually went to a dentist in recent years (usually within the last three or four, as dental records are often purged), and if we know which dentist they might have used. Most people who are discovered decomposed were done so because they have no one very close to them in their life, and therefore no one close enough to them to know who their dentist is.

There's DNA, but that's super expensive, takes far too long to get results, and a last resort in most cases.

If your x-rays at the office reveal the person has some old broken bones, you can search local hospital radiology labs to see if any might have x-rays to compare. But that's more like a fishing expedition half the time. Often old breaks like that happened years and years earlier anyway.

So that leaves the tried and true method that works just as well on non-decomposed bodies—good old-fashioned fingerprint comparison. Of course, once again, that depends on if the victim ever had fingerprints taken in the past with which to compare. But that's not even the biggest challenge when it comes to using fingerprint comparison to identify someone who's decomposed. The biggest issue goes back to those big, nasty gas blisters I mentioned earlier.

I'm going to simplify all this for a number of reasons, but

as those blisters burst it tears the remaining skin. Because the body is breaking down, skin no longer clings to the body the way it used to and begins to slough away from the limbs. Once that outer layer of skin peels away, so do any prints that existed on the fingers. Even if their fingers still have their skin, and the ridges that create prints, it can be an issue. Because as you ink those fingers up and begin to roll them on the ten-print cards, the epidermis often breaks away and begins slipping and sliding along the finger. You can't get a good enough grip on the finger to transfer the print with ink.

So what's a clever death investigator to do?

Thankfully, there are far more clever investigators out there than me, because once, someone really smart came up with a brilliant idea for this scenario: let that 'skin slippage', as it's called, work for you. The solution is as simple as it is gross.

Now, let's get back to the story and I'll share this clever little solution with you.

Story Continued

When I unzipped the bag, I understood immediately why Bob had been so glib about his request. The guy inside was decomposing in the worst way. Maggots inched their way up and down his body, congregating around the orifices of his face and along the folds of his neck. He was still clothed, yet his shirt and pants buttons were bursting at the seams due to bloating. His face was swollen and nearly jet black, and his tongue protruded from his mouth like a giant slug.

I winced at the foul odor that exploded from the enclosed space, automatically raising my arm to protect my nose.

I looked him up and down. His arms, visible below his short-sleeve shirt, were swelled up with blisters, and I knew the moment I touched them they were going to pop. Though his skin was intact it wouldn't be for long, and that was going to make for some mighty messy fingerprint-taking. I knew the normal way of printing—simply pressing an ink pad to each digit of the hand, then rolling the fingers over a card—wasn't going to work. His skin was too fragile. Turn a finger wrong, and the epidermis around the tips was going to tear.

I'd heard of an alternative way to take fingerprints like this, but I'd never attempted it. Never been trained to do it, either. But I had a feeling this was precisely why Bob had asked me to do them. It was a test of sorts. He wanted to see if I could do it. I planned on not disappointing him.

After gathering the supplies I would need, I set to work.

I slipped some latex gloves over my hands, grabbed a fresh scalpel, and began making light cuts around the top layer of skin near the wrist. It didn't take much effort, but it required a steady hand to ensure a clean cut with no tears. After a few minutes, I'd succeeded in removing the skin of the hand. In effect, I now held a glove made entirely of human skin. Four fingers and a thumb. I even managed to keep the palm in tip-top shape, too.

Carefully, I slid the human-skin glove on to my own hand. After a few minutes to mentally deal with the fact that were a few maggots wriggling around in my hand, I grabbed my right index finger with my left hand to ensure the skin wouldn't slip around, inked it up, and rolled it across the fingerprint card.

A perfect impression of the deceased person's index

finger materialized when I had finished. I continued until all five digits were printed, then did the same thing with the left hand.

In the end, we managed to get an identification on the deceased from an excellent set of fingerprints that I had taken using my own hand in the grossest of ways. I have to admit it's a technique I've gotten much better at over the years, but I will never feel as elated as I did that very first time.

Who are you putting on?

Can you imagine putting on another person's skin, and becoming—for all intents and purposes—that other person? The ink didn't know I wasn't the dead man when I rolled my fingertips across the ten-print card. No fingerprint database could have ever told the difference between my fingers and the dead man's. Although I used my own muscles, tendons, bones, and motor functions...although my finger was very much my own...the prints that resulted were that of the dead man. My identity at that moment was that of the decomposing corpse on that metal table in the morgue.

I had hidden who I was by slipping on someone else.

On the surface it sounds gross, like something straight out of *The Silence of the Lambs*. But on a more spiritual level, it's an amazing picture of what Christ does for us when we give ourselves to Him fully.

See, here's the cold hard truth of things. God is unable to look upon sin. Or rather, a better way to put that would be to say that sin is unable to be in the full presence of God. His purity...His holiness...would eradicate sin the moment it came into contact with Him.

The nature of humans, however, *is* sin. It's not about our actions. It's not about the things we do or don't do. It's that our very DNA is infected with the disease of Sin, with a capital 'S'. It permeates our every molecule. It is a condition we have inherited from our parents and our parents inherited from theirs. It's a genetic disorder that traces all the way back to the first man and woman. Sin corrupted our gene pool, and there was nothing we could do about it.

God, however, wants a relationship with us. He wants to be with us. Wants to spend eternity with us. But because of our inherent Sin nature, we're unable to do so. To step into His presence would obliterate us. Our sin is the great barrier between us and the Creator of all that is. And there is absolutely nothing we can do about it. No matter how much we try to clean ourselves up, we're still stained with Sin. No matter how many good works we do, our countenance is corrupted. No matter how many towers we build, we can never build high enough to reach Him.

Thankfully, He had a plan in Jesus.

He sent His Son, Jesus, to take our place. As the offspring of a virgin, the genetic curse of sin was broken, and the baby Jesus was born pure and without defect. He then lived a perfect life, never sinning once in his entire thirty-three years of life. Being Man, he was able to be tempted, just as we are. Being God, He was able to resist those temptations like we cannot. And then He took our punishment on the cross at Calvary.

Bear in mind, it wasn't the brutal beating and humiliation of the Roman execution that was the worst of the punishment. That was bad, but people have gone through worse. It was the fact that Christ had lived in perfect union with God His entire life. He had never known a moment without feeling God's presence in His life. Had never known what it was like to experience the doubt of God's omnipresence and love. But something happened to Him when Jesus' hands were nailed to that splintered piece of lumber on that barren hill near Jerusalem. Something unbearable. Something truly horrific.

The perfect Man brought all of our sin upon Himself, and God had to turn away from Him. Sin cannot endure God's presence, and now that Christ was full of sin He, too, could not endure God's presence. So while He hung upon that old filthy, blood-stained cross, God stepped out of the picture. Jesus was left utterly alone.

In 2 Corinthians 5:21, Paul describes this as Jesus became "sin for us, so in Him we might become the righteousness of God."

Jesus, who had never sinned, actually became our sin. And why? As Paul points out, it was so that we might become righteous in God's sight.

See, the moment we trust in Christ...the moment we give ourselves to Him completely...He wraps our sin-stained flesh up in his own perfect skin, and our identities are transformed. We are no longer sinful beings in God's sight. We become His children. Our identities change. Just as my own identity through my fingerprints were changed by placing that dead man's skin on my fingertips, Christians are covered up with the purity of Christ when we trust in Him and make Him Lord of our lives.

Paul would agree with my sentiment here as well. In Galatians 3:27, he tells us, "For as many of you as were baptized into Christ, have put on Christ." And in Romans

12:14, he says, "But put on the Lord Jesus Christ, and make no provision for the flesh, to gratify its desires."

By the way, that second verse is pretty powerful. It tells us that not only are we as Christians putting on the identity of Christ when we trust in Him, but that by doing so we're given the power to overcome our sinful nature. Paul wouldn't have commanded us to 'make no provision for the flesh' if we didn't have the ability of overcome it. Without an identity in Christ, we have no hope of this. But in Christ, we most certainly do.

Who are you wearing?

Do you ever watch those Hollywood award shows like the Academy Awards or the Emmys? Ever see those beautiful celebrities waving and smiling at the flashing cameras, being peppered with questions by reporters and paparazzi?

All too often the most common question you'll hear is, "Who are you wearing?" What they're really being asked is, "Who designed your clothes?" These awards shows are pretty big deals for actors, musicians, and celebrities of all kinds, so they spend tons of money at clothing labels to impress. And the press eats it up. So, instead of questions about the movies or TV shows they're associated with, reporters tend to make big deals over the fashions seen as these events.

Why is this? What does it matter what designer made these people's clothes?

It's really all about status. You'll never hear a celeb admitting to getting their suit from Sears or Walmart. Heck, they'd never admit to buying their suit from Men's

Warehouse either. No, if they want to impress, they have to get the very best that fashion has to offer. They take great pride, as the cameras snap, of telling everyone who they're wearing because it means, in their eyes anyway, that they made it. Clothing is status, just as much as the cars they drive or the houses they live in.

While I'm personally not a big fan of this notion, I have to admit that it's true for us as well. Who we are wearing—spiritually—is very much a status symbol for us as well. Only, for us it's the difference between freedom and slavery.

Who are you wearing? Are you wearing the world? Are you wearing your sinful nature? Are you stuck in the flesh? I have news for you. Although you may feel as though you are free of all the 'rules', and free to do as you please with no repercussions, you are, in fact, a slave to sin. You can't help it. You have no control over it. Sin dominates you, and you cannot, of your own power, break away.

But if you're wearing Christ, you are a whole new being! You have a whole new identity. You are no longer a slave to anything, but are truly free. In fact, God doesn't see you as one of His fallen creatures anymore. The moment you put on Christ, you become His child. The Apostle John tells us that 'but as many as received Him (Jesus), to them He gave the right to become children of God' (John 1:12)!

Now that's some status!

If you have put on Christ, take heart in this. Rejoice in the fact that your identity has changed. And know that, with it, you are no longer who you used to be and now have the power to overcome that genetic condition we call sin.

11
THAT'S NEVER COMING OUT OF YOUR CARPET

CASE # 16-0301
DECEDENT: REDACTED, Regina
Re: Unattended Death

I knew something was strange the moment I pulled up to 423 Beardley Lane and saw water streaming from underneath the closed garage door. But I'll be honest—I really had no idea how strange the scene was going to be. Sure, the detective had given me a brief overview over the phone when he'd called me about the case. But if there's anything I've learned in all my years on the job, it's that cops typically don't like 'icky', and they tend to exaggerate when a case is veering in that direction.

In this particular situation, however, Detective Rodriguez hadn't exaggerated. If anything, he hadn't described it horrifically enough. But that's life in the death investigation game. A prize in every case.

"Thanks for getting out here so quickly," Rodriguez said,

stomping up to my car. I noticed he was wearing his wader boots.

I glanced down at them, then looked him in the eyes. "It's that bad in there?"

He nodded to the steady stream of water still trickling down from the car port. "That's nothing," he said. "Wait until you see inside."

I sighed, then walked over to my trunk and grabbed my equipment. Unfortunately, I hadn't brought my own waders, so my work uniform boots were going to have to do. "Lead the way." I gestured toward the house.

We approached the front porch, and Rodriguez started filling me in on the details. "Neighbors hadn't seen our victim in about a week. Maybe longer." He opened the front door. I could see the carpeting in the living room was soaked with water. There was probably a full inch of water covering the entire first floor of the house. "Then this morning, one of the neighbors…" He glanced down at his notes. "A John Miller… happened to notice the water coming from the garage door, and became concerned. He called us, and we came out to investigate. Everything was locked up tight, so deputies broke out a back window, and made the discovery."

I stepped inside, and was instantly greeted by an unnerving slurp from the carpet. Once near the middle of the living room, I glanced around. My initial assessment had been spot-on. The water had risen to about an inch high—in all directions. But that wasn't the disturbing part. No, what made my stomach roil at that moment was the occasional splotches of shimmering yellow that floated within the water throughout the room—like a river of butter.

"Is that…"

"Yup."

I shuddered, crouching down for a better look at the Yellow. "And how long has she not been seen?"

Rodriguez shrugged. "Neighbors weren't sure, but they said it has definitely been longer than a week."

I took a few sniffs, but could smell little more than mold. Nothing of the foul stench I would have expected on a normal case like this. I then turned my attention back to the Yellow. My gloved finger dipped into the water just above the carpet's surface, and swirled around. The Yellow swirled with it.

"Okay," I said. "Let's have a look at her."

Rodriguez choked back his revulsion with a nod, then started making his way toward the back of the house and the master bedroom. The carpet seemed even more saturated as we approached. The Yellow was now more concentrated, clumping together in congealed masses here and there. I tiptoed over them, working hard to avoid stepping anywhere near the Yellow. But it was purely psychological. My boots were irreparably contaminated now. There was nothing that could be done for them.

We moved into the bedroom, then through the doorway leading to the master bath. This room was tiled. The mirrors were fogged, and the temperature was considerably higher in there than the rest of the house. The clumps of Yellow were even thicker here, and rolled back and forth as our feet sloshed through the water.

"The water was still on?" I asked.

The detective nodded. "Deputies turned the shower off when they found her."

I stepped over to the walk-in shower and opened the glass door. My victim—or what was left of her anyway—lay on the shower floor. Much of her bones were now exposed. Her hands, feet, and much of her torso were stripped of flesh. If it had been the work of a murderer or animal, the carnage wouldn't have been nearly as disturbing to me as the horrific truth of what I was looking at. What I knew in my mind was true despite my plaintive pleas to the contrary. But there was no denying the truth.

As I glanced down at her body, then over at the clumps of Yellow still floating around the rest of the house, I knew precisely what had happened.

Sometime—more than a week ago—this poor lady had stripped down and gotten into the shower, just as she had done a million times before. And she had died. Whether it was a heart attack or a slip and fall, she had gone down in that large walk-in shower and never stood up again.

But the water had continued to pour from the showerhead. The water heater had continued to do its job, and had pumped more and more hot water down on top of her. Minutes had turned to hours. Hours to days. Days to at least a week. And still that water had poured on her. And over time, it began to erode her body. Over time, it had begun to cause her body to literally melt. The skin sloughed away and the fat fell apart, to be washed away by the overflow throughout the rest of the house.

You see, the Yellow I was so concerned with from the moment I stepped into the poor woman's house was her adipose. Her fat. The water had stripped it from her body, and washed it away from her forever.

Under Pressure

Ever heard that song by David Bowie, 'Under Pressure'? Most of us have. It's a fantastic song. Classic '80s. In it, Bowie talks about the pressure we all face in life and its effects on our lives. In the song, he describes pressures in life as 'terrors'. Pressures, according to Bowie, chip around and kick our brains. It tears families in two. It brings buildings down. We watch our friends screaming, "Let me out!" And there's nothing we can do for them because we have the very same pressures as they do.

Bowie's prescription for this problem? It seems to be either to love more and harder, or go insane. Personally, I prefer the former to the latter. I'm pretty sure you do, too.

Our lady in the case above was no longer feeling the pressure of life when she died. She was free of it completely. But her body...that's another matter entirely. Her body continued to feel the pressure of the shower water as it rained down on her. It bubbled at the pressure of heat. It bloated up from the pressure of gases building up inside her. Until, eventually, she was worn away to nothing.

Her body quite literally melted into the carpet. It eroded away.

Pressure can do that. It erodes our beaches. When hurricanes come the pressure builds and eats away at land, often leaving many people homeless or at least in need of major repairs. Pressure causes the bends within our bodies if we are scuba diving and ascend too quickly. In fact, pressure can crush us completely if we dive too deep. Pressure waves from an explosion can decimate buildings that aren't even within a bomb's range. It can bring down bridges. Pressure from two cars colliding can mangle our heaps of metal and fiberglass as if they are little more than tinfoil.

And that's just physical pressure. Emotional and spiritual pressure can be even more powerful. Even more destructive. As the song says, it can tear families apart. It can bankrupt us. It can end lives. And, unfortunately, there's very little we can do to avoid it. Pressures are, unfortunately, a part of life.

If you live in this world, then you will eventually find yourself in some sort of crisis. Medical, financial, marital. These crises are most common, and with them comes pressures we can never prepare for. Pressures that threaten to crush us. To melt us into sludge. To erode our faith and joy.

Embrace the Pressure

So pressure sounds bad, right? It's destructive. It hurts us. It causes so many problems. The best way to deal with pressure is simply to avoid it, right? Oh, if only it was as simple as that.

David Bowie's song talks about that, too. He talks about people who 'sat on a fence', trying to avoid the pressures the world has to offer. But, as he points out, it just doesn't work. If you live in this world—if you interact with people or have a job or responsibilities of any kind—you're going to have to face pressures.

But here's the good news! Pressure isn't always bad. It often produces amazing things.

Pressure melts away carbon from chunks of coal, but in doing so it creates priceless diamonds. Water pressure chipped away at the thousands of tons of rock, and over time it left us with the Grand Canyon. Some of the greatest innovations of modern times have come about from people under pressure—space missions, anyone?

Of course, there's also my personal favorite...my mom used to use a pressure cooker to make incredibly tender and tasty pot roast dinners.

Point is, it's not the pressure itself that's destructive. It's how we handle the pressure that's the key. Our dead woman in the shower only floated out into the carpet of her house because her drain clogged up. If we allow the pressures of our life to clog us up, we're going to fall apart. We're going to be torn to shreds. Our marriages are going to fail, and our finances are going to fall into ruin.

But God uses pressure for many things in our lives. He uses it to teach us to rely on Him when things get tough. Everyone has heard that old saying, "God never gives us more than we can handle". Most people think that's from the Bible. Most people would be wrong. In fact, it's not theologically true at all.

God often allows more trouble to fall on our shoulders than we can possibly handle. He heaps it on us. Why would He do this? Because He wants to carry the burden on our behalf. He wants us to rely on Him throughout our everyday lives—when things are good and when things are bad. But all too often, when things go smoothly for us, we tend to forget about Him. We put our lives on cruise control, and drive through life on our own power. So God turns up the pressure. The pressure is our invitation to join Him in the miracles of our lives.

We'd do well to embrace those hard times in our lives, because that's precisely when God does His mightiest works through us.

12

THE RAT SHANTY

CASE # 11-0047
DECEDENT: REDACTED, Marcus
Re: Undetermined Death

I pulled up onto the shoulder of State Road A1A and got out of my car. There were several patrol cars, at least one unmarked detective car, and a crime scene unit parked along the side of the road with me, but no human in sight. I looked around, searching for a contact person, but all I saw was the dense vegetation of a Florida jungle all around me.

Grabbing my camera and notebook, I inched closer to the edge of the vegetation and peered past the palmetto bushes in front of me. I couldn't see anything through the dense foliage. Couldn't hear anything either.

"Hello?" I shouted, but got no response.

I walked over to the nearest patrol car, and peered through the darkly tinted windows. No one was inside.

Sheesh. Where is everyone?

The Rat Shanty | 113

I straightened up at the sound of tires crunching into the dirt behind me and turned around. A big red fire engine had just arrived. I scratched my head at this. There was no fire, and the guy I had come to investigate was clearly dead—at least from the conversation I'd had with Detective Newton on the phone. He was decomposing, in fact.

Four fully-dressed firefighters slid out from the truck and set to work gathering their equipment. Curious, I walked up to the battalion chief.

"What are you guys doing here?" I asked him with a nod of greeting. We'd worked together a few times in the past, but mostly during traffic fatalities where his crew had to cut decedents out of mangled vehicles.

"They called us out here," the chief said. "Apparently, they can't get to the body. Need us to cut him out."

"Cut him out..."

Before I could finish my question, Detective Newton stalked out of the wood line. She was a petite blonde, and struggled to step over the undergrowth to get to us.

"Glad you guys are here," she said, waving to us.

I already knew about the case. There wasn't much to it. Just a homeless guy in the woods. Some hunters had stumbled upon his little shanty, and had smelled something foul. When they looked inside to investigate, they'd found his corpse. There wasn't anything suspicious. The death looked natural enough. But, like most transients in the area, he had no known treating physician to sign his death certificate. That's why I was involved.

"Okay, here's the deal," Newton said, waving for us to follow. We stepped into the jungle, and she continued to talk. "Our guy has built a pretty elaborate hut out here, and we just can't get to him. We need you guys..." She was now talking to the fire chief. "...to cut him out of the hut."

I heard the firefighters behind me grunting as they lugged the heavy cutting equipment through the foliage. There was no path that I could discern. Everything was overgrown with vines, brambles, and large prehistoric-looking leaves. The deeper into the woods we moved the more obstacles we encountered, and the hotter it got. After several hundred yards in, I could see a few deputies meandering up ahead. An old metal structure came into view as well.

"He's inside," Newton answered my unspoken question.

As we approached, I quickly gained a better view of the lean-to structure. The guy who'd built it had spent a great deal of time constructing something sturdy. Maybe even hurricane-proof. It was comprised of five large sheets of corrugated metal, with a narrow door cut into one of the walls.

The path to the structure was clear of debris, and I noticed a broom resting against the side of the building. Apparently, the resident of the place liked to sweep away the dirt from the dirt around his domicile while he was alive. In fact, as far as homeless camps go, this was by far the neatest and least cluttered I'd ever seen.

"There's nothing suspicious," Newton said, gesturing toward the door. "Lots of beer cans inside, so the guy's a drinker."

I squeezed into the opening and looked around. The place was cramped. The ceiling hung very low, and even at five-foot-six-inches-tall I was forced to stoop in order to move around. In the shadows of the confined space, there was no way I could get a good look at the man. We'd have to get him out before I could do any sort of examination. But now I understood the reasoning behind calling the engine to the scene. There just wasn't enough space inside to even begin to drag him out into the light. The only way to get him out would be to cut down the shelter that had protected him from the elements.

After a few moments, I stepped back out into the daylight and was forced to blink. I hadn't realized how dim it had been inside. Then again, the only light available came from the extremely narrow door space.

Once I had regained my equilibrium, the firefighters set to work cutting a rectangular hole near the base of the hut. While they worked, my transport crew arrived and prepared their stretcher and body bag in anticipation of freeing the body from its metal sarcophagus. After about ten minutes I heard a loud cracking sound above the high-pitched whine of the saw, and knew the firefighters were nearly finished.

Another minute or two and the saw's motor shut off, filling the air with an almost deafening silence. I shifted from one foot to the other, growing bored with waiting. One of the firefighters retrieved a crowbar, and set to work on breaking the now-sawed panel away from the rest of the structure. With several large metallic cracks, the panel fell away and...

My eyes widened at the sight of what must have been dozens (at the time, it look more like thousands) of rats cascading out of the little shanty like a tidal wave. The furry creatures tumbled over each other, truly resembling some sort of tsunami as they writhed and wriggled to free themselves from the bleak shelter they had only recently called home. Then, as if of one collective mind, the army of rats dashed toward us, racing over and past our feet and into the woods behind us. We stood stock still for nearly a good two minutes as the rats continued to run past us, and all I could do was watch in horror at the living waterfall that swept by my booted feet.

Three Blind Mice

This event reminded me of the old nursery rhyme 'Three Blind Mice', for some strange reason. In the old song, first put to paper in 1609, the three mice, who happened to be blind, were annoying the old farmer's wife. Annoyed, she grabbed a carving knife, chased them down, and cut off their tails. There are, of course, numerous variations to the song, and some children's books have gone to add to the mice's stories, making them great adventurers who were, in fact, blinded by the farmer's wife while running into a patch of brambles to get away from her.

Throughout the centuries, people have tried to draw deeper meaning or symbolism from the song, but nothing adds up historically to make sense of it. I've pretty much always figured that this song is exactly what it is—a fun children's song that can be sung in rounds. And also, the theme to the Three Stooges...but that's another story entirely.

But as I watched that tsunami of rats tumbling across the ground toward my feet, the Three Blind Mice song is exactly what went through my head. Well, after my initial "Oh crap!" reaction, anyway.

Looking back, I think the association is appropriate for much deeper reasons than the obvious. Yes, it was multiple rats—or mice. Does anyone really know the difference when they're barreling toward you in droves?—frolicking through a forest. That's enough in itself to foster association with the song. But there's something else there, too.

The notion of blindness. The scurrying out of the shadows into the light of day. The fleeing from observers.

It reminded me of something else, too. It reminded me of sin.

Now I know, we fallen humans don't like to talk much about sin these days. It makes us uncomfortable. Many will say such talk is negative, and will turn people away from God. Lots of preachers out there tend not to bring it up in their sermons if they can help it. It just seems so judgmental to even whisper the word out loud.

In fact, if we could, we'd lock the very notion of sin up in its own little dark prison where no one can even see it. We'd try to forget it was there if it was possible to do so. We'd tie up those nasty little sins, toss them into a metal crate, wrap chains around the box, and throw it into the deepest depths of the sea if it were possible. But it's not possible.

So we continue to sin, and shove that sin somewhere in the back of our little metal shed, hoping no one will notice. Hoping no one will ever see. We want to be blind to our sin. Even more, we hope the world will be blind to the sin we've hidden away.

Three blind mice.

See how they run.

Here's the thing about sin: it can't be contained. It can't be hidden for long. Sooner or later, something comes along that saws open the prison we've shoved our sins into and they run out into the light. They scatter. They scurry.

Did ever you see such a sight in your life?

They run over people's feet in a tidal wave of filth. And people can't help but notice. They can't help but see your dirty little secrets darting into the light, looking for the nearest block of shadow to hide within. But it's too late now. Your sin is exposed. Your secrets have been let out of their cage. Your shame is evident to everyone.

If we hide sin, it is inevitable that it will escape. We will be exposed.

"...and you may be sure that your sin will find you out." (Numbers 32:23b)

So what can be done about it? Are you doomed to have your most embarrassing qualities—those little favorite sins you just can't seem to deal with—bring you down? Are you destined to have these sins ruin your life?

Not at all! There's hope! Although it's not going to be easy.

...Good for the soul

Solomon knew a little something about sin, and the consequences of trying to conceal them from the world. His father, David, knew it better than probably anyone as well. Both men—Godly men who sought after righteousness as much as anyone possibly can—were very, very flawed. Both men had their particular vices. And both men sinned magnificently.

In Proverbs 28:13, Solomon talks about the consequences of trying to cover up these sins. "Whoever conceals their sins does not prosper..." Whoa. Sounds pretty grim, doesn't it? And it seems to confirm what I've been saying all along in this chapter. Sin cannot be contained. It'll come out eventually. No matter how many lies you weave to camouflage or conceal it, our evil deeds will be revealed and it will lead to our ruin if left unchecked.

Fortunately, that's not the end of that verse. Solomon goes on to say, "...but the one who confesses and renounces them finds mercy."

Ah! There's the key. There's the answer. Confession. Repentance. These two things are our safeguard against the ruin that comes from our habitual sin.

Confession is a big one, too. Ever notice the feeling you get when you come clean with someone after you've done them wrong? Ever notice that instant feeling of relief you get? That sensation that thousands of pounds have been lifted off your chest? There's nothing quite like it.

James 5:16 says, "Therefore confess your sins to each other and pray for each other so that you may be healed." Healing starts with confession. It only makes sense that it would ease the burden once we've expressed our wrongdoing, and asked to be forgiven of it. It's the very first step in clearing out that old metal shed filled with the rats of sin. Confess. Feel better. Be healed.

But notice that Solomon didn't stop with confession in Proverbs 28:13. He also tells us that we have to 'renounce' our sins as well. Another word for that is 'repent'. A less Sunday-School word for that is to 'turn away from' our sin. It's all well and good to admit that we have sinned. It's great, and is the beginning of our healing and cleansing. But simply confessing that we've done wrong isn't enough.

In order to empty out that disease-ridden rats' nest of our souls, we also have to repent from it. We have to turn away from it. Put it out of our lives for good. In Peter's first big sermon (Acts 3), he tells everyone to "Repent, then, and turn to God, so that your sins may be wiped out, that times of refreshing may come from the Lord."

In order for our sins to be 'wiped out'—stricken from the record—we must repent. We must turn away from them. Confess, and turn away from our sins, and those nasty old rats will go away like they never existed. It's as simple as that.

"But Kent," you might be saying, "I've tried. I've tried so hard to stop [insert personal sin here], and I just can't do it." Well, yes, you can. Sin has no power over you if you belong to Christ. But it'll take time. It'll take patience. And most importantly, it'll take self-forgiveness. Christ has and always will forgive you. Always know that. But a lot of times, we're our own worst critic. We try and try and try to stop committing our little pet sins, and we keep failing and failing and failing. And we beat ourselves up over it. We feel ashamed of it. And the cycle starts all over by us trying to hide them away all over again.

Stop beating yourself up over it. This whole sanctification process (the process of becoming more and more holy) is a marathon, not a sprint. God changes us gradually over time. And, over time, it becomes easier and easier to avoid the sins we enjoyed in the past. They key to it all is in that second phrase in Peter's sermon I mentioned a few paragraphs up: "Repent, then, and turn to God..."

And turn to God.

That's it. It's as simple as that. Stop focusing on your sins, and focus on Him. Turn your thoughts and mind away from your failures, and look to Christ's successes. Seek Him first in everything, and everything else will fall into place (Matthew 6:33). Don't sweat it. That rats' nest will be cleared out eventually. But while you're working on it, remember what

James said: "Come near to God and He will come near to you." (James 4:8).

If you approach Christ every day, I guarantee you'll find those little disease-ridden vermin fleeing from your path on a daily basis. Just trust God at His word, and you'll be amazed at the progress you'll see in your life.

MEATLOAF IS MURDER

CASE # 15-0215
DECEDENT: REDACTED, Vernon
Re: Homicide

I sighed as I climbed out of my car and looked at the quaint little ranch-style home at the end of the cul-de-sac. I was going to a homicide. And despite what you might think, homicides are usually the most boring cases a guy in my line of work can investigate. They usually involved drug deals gone bad, gangbangers getting their colors, or husbands beating their wives to death in a drunken rage. As Sherlock Holmes often lamented in Doyle's stories, criminals had no sense of imagination. And the average murder was just that...average.

I wasn't looking forward to the case at all as I trudged up the sidewalk to the front door and knocked. As I waited for someone to answer, I gave the front of the house a quick once-over. The yard was neatly manicured. The flower bed lining the exterior was neatly pruned, and the flowers were in full bloom and well taken care of. The front door and shutters were white, and shone in the moonlight crisply, without a speck of dirt.

While the neighborhood was distinctly low income, it seemed quiet and hospitable. The kind of neighborhood that was older, with older residents who took great pride in the community's appearance. The house I'd come to investigate seemed no different. It definitely wasn't your typical drug house or gang domicile.

So, it's got to be abuse, I thought to myself just as the door swung open and a uniformed deputy offered a nod of greeting. *Domestic bliss turned deadly.*

I was about to find out that I was half-right, but my preconceived notions couldn't have prepared me for the strange case of Mrs. Nelson and the Meatloaf Dinner.

The deputy gestured for me to come inside. He then stepped out behind me, leaving me in the meager living room that was just as neat and tidy as any grandmother's home you'd ever stepped into. Detectives Jarvis and Gaines stood with the crime scene technician in the kitchen. When they saw me, they finished their hushed conversation and walked over to me. I ignored them as I moved immediately over to the body of an elderly man lying in the center of the room on the floor. I could already tell from the bloody holes in his otherwise clean white shirt that he had been shot multiple times.

Gaines opened his mouth to fill me in on the story, but I held up a hand. This case had already garnered my interest. I knew right away it had nothing to do with drugs. And if abuse was involved, it wasn't apparent. This was an interesting homicide, I could sense it, and I wanted to try my hand at deducing what happened without the benefit of the detectives' foreknowledge. I wanted to put my Sherlock Holmes skills to another test yet again.

Truth is, when I do this, it only works about thirty percent of the time, if that. After all, Sherlock Holmes is a fictional character. So is Monk. And so is Shawn Spencer of *Psych*, my favorite detective show. Their methods don't really work in real life. There are just too many variables to consider in any murder scene. But it doesn't mean I don't like giving it a try whenever I can anyway.

I spent a few minutes looking the old man up and down, counting the bullet wounds, tracing the blood spatter, and imagining what had happened to lead him to his current position. I imagined him sitting in the recliner directly behind his body. I pictured his killer walking up to him, and firing down. I could see him standing in surprise just as more bullets ripped through him, the impact whirling him around, where he was shot a few more times in the back before collapsing to the floor.

I offered my hypothesis to the detectives, who nodded their agreement. Apparently, their suspect had already told them what happened.

"It was his wife," Detective Jarvis said. "She called us after killing him. Flat out told dispatch she'd killed him. When we got here she was sitting over there on the couch, her hands out and ready to be handcuffed. It was weird. She was so matter of fact about the whole thing. She told us again that she had killed him, and fully expected to be arrested for it."

I shook my head. Kind of sad that a little old lady—in her late seventies from what the detectives told me—would be spending the rest of her life in jail. But now I was curious as to the 'why' of it all. I was tempted to just ask the detectives, but it would spoil the fun for me. I wanted to press on with my Sherlock experiment and see how far I could take it.

I had already spent quite a bit of time in the living room and had seen nothing there that shed light on the wife's motives for killing her husband of fifty-two years. I noticed that the crime scene technician was still busy in the kitchen, and figured that was the next best place to look.

Careful where I stepped, I moved to the doorway leading into the kitchen, pushed open the saloon-style doors, and stepped into what I can only describe as the 1970s. The floor was lined with pea-soup green and brown linoleum that had begun curling up at the corners of the room. The cabinets were oak and dark brown. Wood paneling covered the walls, giving the kitchen a dark, dingy appearance. An old metal kitchen table sat to my left, half-eaten portions of food still sat in the center. A broken plate lay scattered on the floor near the table legs. A few pieces of the plate had been placed back on the table, but the majority remained on the linoleum.

I moved away from the dining area, and directly over to the stove and kitchen sink. There were pots and pans, now cold, on the stove. A cookbook—from the looks of it, it was for gourmet cuisine and brand spanking new—sat open next to the sink. I read the recipe. It was for what looked to be a pretty fancy dish. It was something akin to meatloaf, but I couldn't pronounce what it was actually called. This was not the kind of meal my mom would make, but something much more suave and sophisticated. If it had a French name, I wouldn't have been surprised.

What I did know about the meal was that it would have taken a lot of time and love to make.

I glanced over at the table and the broken plate, then at the cookbook and stove.

"Oh, you've got to be kidding me," I muttered as the story came together in my head. I looked over at the detectives, who had crossed their arms in amusement at me while they watched me piece it all together. It wasn't difficult. All the clues were right there for anyone to see. You didn't have to be Sherlock Holmes to figure this one out. "So the husband was a jerk, wasn't he?"

The detectives nodded. "From what we understand, yeah," Jarvis said.

"Hold on," said Gaines. "What do you think happened here?"

I shrugged, point to the cookbook. "Your suspect tried to do something special for her husband," I said. "Wanted to cook him something nice. Something different. She slaved away over the stove for hours, preparing this great supper, and he..."

"He wasn't happy with it," Jarvis said. "Yeah. As a matter of fact, he's the one who threw the plate on the floor. She started to pick it up, but then stopped. She just got so mad."

The detectives filled me on the rest of the story. Apparently, after Mrs. Nelson had stopped picking up the mess her husband had made, she had stormed off into their bedroom. The husband, still angry over his wife's failed meal, had gone into the living room and sat down in his favorite chair to watch some TV. A few minutes later the wife came out into the living room with her husband's gun, and started shooting him right there on the spot. She'd emptied the weapon into him, then calmly called the police, took her seat on the couch, and waited for the cops to arrive to arrest her.

From all accounts, while the husband had been a difficult

man, there'd never been any accusations of abuse. The wife denied he'd ever been abusive toward her at all. She'd just felt so slighted by his indifference to the supper she'd prepared, she'd snapped. Picked up her husband's own gun, and shot him with it until he was dead. And then some.

Pat on the back

We all like to feel appreciated. While the result of hard work can often be its own reward, there's nothing quite like the feeling of a pat on the back from people whose opinions we respect, and covet.

In my own job, I get a great sense of pleasure when the medical examiner tells me I've done a good job, or commends me for seeing something everyone else missed. There's a thrill to it. An adrenaline rush. Endorphins kick in, and you get a sense of peace from it.

Psychologists have been talking about this for years. Pavlov and his dogs. Jung. Even Freud. Positive reinforcement to foster positive behavior. We do good, we expect rewards. Appreciation, we find, is the greatest of all rewards in our social circles.

When I was a kid, if I mowed the yard without being told to do so I would make sure my parents knew before they even got home from work. The implication being that I wanted praise for my initiative and hard work. It was a bit mercenary, I admit, but it was also very, very human.

Psych!

But what happens when we don't get those pats on the back? What happens when you don't get the recognition at work that you deserve? What happens when the ones we're closest to take our hard work for granted? It happens more often than we care to think about, and it usually leaves a knot in our stomach that we just can't shake.

Your spouse forgets your anniversary. The kids run out the door after supper without so much as a 'thank you'. Your boss has you stay after hours to finish that project, then never even bothers to commend you for it.

When these things happen, we feel like we're taken for granted. We feel unappreciated. Maybe we even feel a little invisible or unloved. Is it too much to ask for recognition? Is it too much for a simple nod of thanks when we go above and beyond? Would it kill your spouse to show gratitude for that dinner you slaved over for hours? It's enough to make some people want to grab a gun and take out their frustrations.

But before you do that, let's stop and think about a few things.

Sometimes, it takes time

I know that's not something we want to hear, but it's very true. Sometimes, appreciation comes over time. My own parents are perfect examples of this. I think they would agree that I was never a 'bad' kid. Well, at least not until my twenties. As a child, though, I was pretty good. I never wanted to disappoint my folks, so I pretty much stayed on the straight and narrow.

But not being a bad kid is a far cry from being a great kid. I had my issues, and I'd say the number one biggie for me was that I rarely appreciated the things my parents did for me growing up.

Examples: Growing up, my dad owned a small used furniture store in our small Kentucky town. Right across the street from him was a high-end furniture store with a budget that included radio commercials every hour, on the hour. Naturally, my dad's business struggled to compete. He was forced to expand the business, and he really made his money fixing vacuum cleaners and sewing machines. Still, he was not a wealthy man. Despite that, however, he tried his best to give his kids the best he possibly could.

As a child, I had a hard time understanding this. When my friends were getting the cool Evel Knievel crank-up motorcycle, I got a cheap plastic knockoff that had no crank and was only propelled by me pushing it along with my hands. It was barbaric!

When my friends were playing Atari, my dad was bringing home an old Pong game he got at a 'scratch and dent' sale. I wouldn't get my first Atari until Nintendo was becoming popular.

Never mind that I had every *Six Million Dollar Man* action figure and play set on the market; it was the things I couldn't have that irked me. And so I moped and groaned about how unfair my life was—even though one Christmas he got me the coolest bicycle in my neighborhood.

And he'd always give me the last bite of steak after our Sunday afternoon lunches, despite the fact that he loved red meat just as much as I did.

I look back at my attitude during those times, and cringe at my selfishness. I've never known a more honest, hardworking man in my whole life than my dad. He's always been someone you could trust at his word, and I know now that he did everything he could to give me the things I wanted. And there's no doubt he always provided the things I needed without question.

It wasn't until my late teenage years to early adulthood that I truly began to appreciate him and all the sacrifices he made for me. He'll never know how much, though our relationship is so tight now that I think he has an inkling. I hope he does anyway.

The same is true with my mom. Oh, the things she did for her kids that my sister and I probably will never even know about. Her incredible cooking—in which she would make sure to make special alternatives for our particular tastes. Her driving us to school every day for years. Helping us with our Halloween costumes, and decorating our spooky haunted house to be even spookier so we could have the coolest house in town.

I think of all the times she sat up with us when we were sick, giving us medicine and taking us to doctor's appointments. She was a working mother during the era of the latchkey kids, but she always made us a priority in everything. And oh, how many times did I make her chase me around the house—running down one staircase and up the back staircase of our Victorian home—for the spanking I definitely deserved. Spankings that were always meted out with a steady hand. Never done in anger. And always explained beforehand why I was getting it.

My parents—who are still together after fifty-odd years—have always been the very best. But their children can't quite say the same. I know growing up that I didn't appreciate them the way I should have.

But I do now. And then some.

Growing up

But that's my point. I took growing up to learn to really appreciate my folks. And while we deal every day with 'grownups' who never seem to appreciate us, we all have spiritual and emotional growing left to do. Don't give up. The people who never seem to appreciate the things you do are still growing. Keep doing what you're doing, no matter what. There will come a time when these people will realize how precious you are to them, and they'll show it.

And if they don't? Some people just never grow up, right? That's okay, too.

Keep doing what you're doing, no matter how people react to you. No matter how little appreciation you might feel. Because you never know who's watching. You never know who's noticing. While your boss or coworker might be completely blind to the efforts you put into your work, there might be a customer who sees it. There might be another coworker who needs the example you are setting. There might be someone unexpected who benefits from the hard work you do who will appreciate it, and never get the chance to let you know what you mean to them.

Our actions always have consequences. A lot of times, these consequences are unforeseen...not to mention unseen. You never know when a difficult-to-muster smile might change someone's life. You never know when a gentle touch might be the thing that stops someone from ending their own life.

Keep doing what you're doing, no matter how unappreciated you might feel. I can guarantee you one thing...your positive actions and attitude will affect those around you in a positive way. That great meal you cook might not please the one you intended to please, but the ingredients you bought to make it might have put food on a farmer's table that desperately needed it.

Keep doing what you're doing. I promise you, if you do you will get the reward of appreciation you desperately seek eventually. It might not be in this life, but there will be no greater reward, at the end of all things, than to hear Jesus say, "Well done, my good and faithful servant."

Now *that* is appreciation to beat them all, so keep doing what you're doing. No matter what.

14

SALT OF THE EARTH

CASE # 18-0087
DECEDENT: REDACTED, Gerald
Re: Possible Drug Overdose

The house I pulled up to was near the beach. As I stepped out of my car, I took a deep breath of the salt air and stood there for a moment. Normally, I'm not a big fan of the beach. I always feel so sticky after I've spent time around it for some reason, and don't get me started about the heat and the blazing sun. Just not a big fan. But that day was near perfect. The temperature was mild, made even milder with the nice ocean breeze blowing my way.

When I turned to look at the house I was about to enter, my good mood withered real quick. Despite the mega-million-dollar beach houses the average person sees as they drive along State Road A1A, there are portions of the area that are throwbacks to the days before Florida became a major tourist attraction. Old houses. Rickety, dilapidated shacks. Rusted out trailer parks. The beach has them all. The house my dead guy was in wasn't as bad as it could be, but it wasn't pleasant-looking either. Probably built in the early '70s the place was in need of some major repairs, having seen two or three too many hurricanes—not to mention owners who just didn't care.

Of course, knowing that I was here for a possible drug overdose, I hadn't expected anything different really. It's sad to say. I mean, I get overdoses in some of those multi-million-dollar beach houses I mentioned a minute ago, too, but even they are usually falling apart from the inside when I get to them. Drugs have a way of doing that.

The door to the home opened up, and I could see one of the city's uniformed police officers amble down the steps of the front porch. As I approached, he nodded at me in greeting.

"They're inside," he said. "Go on in."

I watched the robust officer wobble over to his car and get into the air conditioning with a sigh. Wiping the smile from my face, I step inside to see two other uniformed officers and a detective standing near the kitchen. I was just about to walk over to them when I noticed a white substance on the floor just at the front door. I bent over to take another look. The substance wasn't a powder. They were fine grains of some kind. I had a feeling I knew exactly what it was, and why it was there, so I continued walking over to the cops in the kitchen.

After the usual hellos, I turned to the detective. "So, what's the story?"

"Owner of the place rents her rooms in the house out to several people," the detective began as he led me down the hallway toward the room the deceased was in. "One of her tenants was found dead in bed this morning. We found needles, a spoon, and a baggie of what looks like heroin on the nightstand of his bed."

"I take it he has a history of drug use?"

As we walked down the hallway, I looked at the doors of each of the rooms we passed. They all had the same line of white at the base of the doors.

The detective nodded. "We've arrested him on drug and alcohol charges a few times."

When we got to the decedent's door, a crime scene tech from the sheriff's office was busy snapping photos and taking measurements. She'd been loaned out to the PD to collect whatever evidence needed collecting.

"Stef," I said to the tech.

"Kent," Crime Scene Tech Stefanie Enoch said with a smile. "Long time, no see."

It was a joke, since I'd only seen her a few hours earlier at another scene.

I pointed down at the white powder at my feet.

"Notice this?" I asked.

She nodded. "It's salt."

"Yeah, I figured." I turned to the detective. "The owner of this place...is she into magic or a psychic or something?"

His eyes widened. "Yeah, she's a Wiccan," he said. "How'd you know?"

"Let me guess, she's not much into drugs or things like that, right?"

"We've got no record on her. And she flat out told me she doesn't like her tenants doing drugs, but there wasn't much she could do to stop them."

I chuckled at this, then nod down at the salt. "Well, she certainly tried."

The detective shook his head. "What do you mean? What does the salt have to do with any of this?"

It's funny. In law enforcement, cops and detectives see all manner of crazy things. Violent things. The worst society has to offer. But there's one thing that they rarely handle very well, and that's magic and the occult. Maybe it's because most cops are rather superstitious, I don't know. But walk into a house with *ngangas* (iron cauldrons with bones and sticks for Palo Mayombe), or Santeria idols, or anything remotely occult, and they kind of shut down. I don't want to say they freak out, but they certainly don't know exactly how to handle things very well.

Because of this deficit, I've spent a great deal of time studying the various magico-religious groups of the Caribbean and other places. Being from the foothills of Appalachia, I'm also pretty well versed in Appalachian folklore and some aspects of hoodoo. In each of these belief systems, salt is always used the same exact way.

To ward off evil spirits.

I explained this to the detective. "You sprinkle a line of salt across the threshold of your front door to keep evil spirits out," I said, then point to the lines of salt all along the doors of the hallway. "I guess the landlady decided she didn't want the evil spirits of her tenants' addictions coming out of their rooms, too, because she's warded their bedroom doors, too."

"You mean..."

"Yeah, she believes the drug addiction is caused by evil spirits," I explained. "The salt was used to keep those spirits out of the main portion of the home."

The detective shuddered at my words. After that we completed our investigation as normal, my crew loaded up the dead man, and we headed back to the medical examiner's office for the autopsy.

Salt and Evil Spirits

It's kind of wild, but almost every culture in every region of the world has the same folkloric beliefs in the power of salt to ward against evil. From the Babylonians to the Israelites, to the Romans, to the Celts, and on through the ages, to the Appalachians, Ozarks, Neo-pagans, and everything in between—salt has been used in some form or another to protect against evil.

Chances are, even you have participated in rituals using salt in this way.

Ever toss a pinch of salt over your left shoulder? Why? Because it's said it brings good luck. Actually, the legends indicate that it doesn't *bring* good luck. It just keeps evil spirits and hexes away from us. But it's such a common practice, even among the most devoted Christians. We do it, and aren't even aware of what we're doing. Nowadays it's merely a quaint custom, and few actually believe it works, but we still practice it.

Older forms of magic would use salt to create protective circles around a magic practitioner while performing rituals. As mentioned in the case above, it was used to line a home's threshold. Farmers would lay salt around feeding troughs to protect their livestock from witches and faeries who enjoyed drying up milk from cattle.

Everywhere we look in human history, salt has played a

major part in protection against evil, hexes, spells, and demons.

Why?

Well, first, prior to the industrial revolution, mining for salt was an arduous and expensive undertaking. During the Roman era, only the richest of the rich could afford salt, which wasn't just used for flavoring their food. It was essential to preserve meat for consumption.

Salt was so valuable that the Romans even paid their soldiers with it. People would turn over their precious gold for the substance.

In religions throughout history, including Judaism, salt was used as a means of purification.

Health-wise, salt is essential to our—and any animal's—existence. It helps regulate hydration, strengthens the nervous system, and balances electrolytes that promote muscle health and flexibility.

Despite its bad press in recent years due to high blood pressure concerns, salt is necessary for our bodies to function right. In essence, it wards off many 'evil' things that might compromise our health.

So for all of its uses as a preservative, a cleanser, a purifier, and a necessary ingredient to stay alive, it only makes sense that such a precious mineral, over time, would gain some sort of metaphysical or supernatural connection. In many ways it's one of the most precious minerals, alongside potassium, in the world today.

Salt Life

There's a very popular marketing brand in Northeast Florida known as 'Salt Life'. You see the stylized logo for 'Salt Life' everywhere you look around here. On bumper and window stickers. On t-shirts. On hats. On every conceivable piece of merchandising you can imagine. There's a Salt Life restaurant, specializing in seafood, as well.

It seems to literally be everywhere around where I live.

The Salt Life philosophy is simple: to embrace the sea and all it has to offer. It's a statement—in fashion and sporting goods—for people who are active in all sorts of water activities from fishing to surfing to scuba diving, and everything in between. It's a way of life for so many people around here, and those who bear the brand find camaraderie wherever they see others sporting the same logo.

There's no question that the Salt Life is appealing. Even a sun-avoiding hermit like me feels drawn to the ocean at times. That salt air I was talking about in the case above... there's nothing quite like it. The sound of the seagulls cawing in mid-flight lures my soul to the freedom the ocean provides.

There's just something about salt that acts as a siren's call to anyone who gets caught in its allure.

I guess that's why Jesus called His followers 'the salt of the earth' (Matthew 5:13). According to Jesus, there's something very special about those who follow Him. Something that should be appealing—appetizing—to the rest of the world. Something about us that offers a bit of spice to an otherwise-bland world. At least, that's how we're supposed to be.

But in the same passage, Jesus also warns about what happens when we lose our saltiness. He explains that once we lose it, we've become useless and should be thrown out. That's not a threat on His part, mind you. It's not an indication that we can lose our salvation or anything like that. It's His way of encouraging us to keep that special zest in our lives. To continue being different from the rest of the world. To provide flavor to an unsavory world.

But I look at the modern church today, and I wonder how tasty we seem to those who aren't Christians. I see us shifting and changing our theology and our practices and our beliefs to fit the rest of the world's menu, and I see us becoming just as bland and sour-tasting as any other group—religious or otherwise—that's out there. We, as the Church, I'm afraid, are losing the spicy quality by striving to meet the tastes of the day. And that's one of the saddest statements I think I've written in this book.

Jesus has warned us not to lose our saltiness. Instead, we're not losing it. We're dissolving it in the water of the world. Don't let it happen to you. If you really want to have that amazing, abundant life we've been talking about since the start of the book, then hold on to your saltiness. Be the spice of life for those around you. Be different. Live a life that makes people crave what you have.

Not only will you live a richer and more fulfilling life for doing so, but you'll be living a life that others want to be part of. You'll be setting an example of the richness that a life in Christ has for everyone.

15

THE CAR CRASH THAT WASN'T

CASE # 13-0242
DECEDENT: REDACTED, Lisa
Re: Traffic Fatality

The flashing police and fire engine lights were nearly blinding as I pulled up at the single-vehicle crash on the secluded two-lane road in the middle of Cracker Swamp. I always hate pulling up to a wreck at night for that very reason. The strobes of red and blue make my retinas dance the Watusi, making it difficult to focus on the road. But, like usual, I managed to pull up to the scene without maiming or killing any troopers walking along the side of the road.

When I got out of my car, I noticed something weird right away.

There weren't any Florida Highway Patrol troopers here at all. Everyone was from the sheriff's office. Very strange, as traffic fatalities in this particular county within my jurisdiction were exclusively jurisdiction of FHP.

I gave a quick look around, and spotted the crashed vehicle to my left. It looked as if it had left the roadway, veered onto the shoulder, and plowed into a guardrail nearly head-on. Pretty cut and dry, really. Maybe that's why the sheriff's office had decided to handle the investigation. Single-vehicle crash. Nothing unusual. Plain and simple. No charges would be filed. Maybe FHP was busy at another wreck, and just couldn't come out to this one.

I shrugged off my questions and sauntered over to the car. Its sole occupant had already been removed from the driver's seat, and was lying on the ground with a sheet covering him or her.

"Hey, Kent," a voice called to me from behind. "Good to see you."

I turned around to see the Lieutenant of Major Crimes, Vinnie Tinnello, walking over to me with a couple detectives I didn't recognize. That wasn't unusual. This particular sheriff's office cycled through detectives like a bladder with an infection. That's not meant to be a gripe against them. It's just that not everyone was able to handle the things Major Crimes had to deal with. Most preferred being on the road as uniformed deputies, or handling simple burglary cases.

Tinnello himself hadn't been with the unit for very long either. Heck, he hadn't been a detective for very long before he made Sergeant, and quickly Lieutenant. The guy was inexperienced, but he was willing to learn and had a good head on his shoulders. I had high hopes for him.

"Vinnie," I said, shaking his hand. "What are you guys doing out here? I figured this would be an FHP case."

He nodded his understanding, then pointed down to our victim.

"Originally, they were. But our deputies got here first, and saw something they found suspicious. So we took jurisdiction, and are working this as a suspicious death."

I looked over at the car, still pressed hard against the guardrail, then back at the lieutenant. I had to force myself not to roll my eyes. I'm a big believer in Occam's Razor—that is, most of the time, the simplest explanation is the right answer.

But because this particular sheriff's office didn't see very many homicides, and didn't quite have the experience as other agencies I worked with, they tended to see murders and suspicions around every corner.

Granted, this is true with any law enforcement agencies no matter how much experience they have. Being a cop means being naturally suspicious. It's the main difference between detectives and a medicolegal death investigator like me. Cops are always asking, "But what if...?" And I'm always asking, "What is the most likely reason things at this scene are the way they are?" I don't deal with 'what ifs'. I deal with evidence, and draw my conclusions from that.

"Really?" I asked. "What sort of suspicions do you guys have?"

Lieutenant Tinnello led me over to the front end of the car. "First of all, there's very little crush damage to the car," he said, pointing at the front bumper. "No braking. No evasive maneuvering. She wasn't going very fast when she struck. It's like she basically just coasted into it."

There was that impulse to roll my eyes again. Instead, I shook my head. "Okay. But it happens all the time. Especially with people with medical issues. She could have had some kind of medical event, went unconscious, and just coasted into the guardrail. It doesn't mean there's anything suspicious going on."

I walked over to the driver's side of the car, where the body lay on the ground. I removed the sheet covering her and looked her over. Part of her face was now discolored from lividity. Her stomach was distended, which was a sign of either early decomposition or CPR attempts. There was a greenish tint to her abdomen, which would seem to corroborate the decomposition hypothesis, but it didn't make sense. There didn't seem to be enough time for her to already be decomposing.

"So tell me again, what happened? Who reported this crash?"

Tinnello cleared his throat, and reviewed his notes. "Passerby. He was traveling north along the road when he spotted the car. Thought it was weird, so he pulled over to check it out. He found our victim slumped over in the driver's seat. She was unrestrained, and leaning over the center console. She wasn't breathing, so he pulled her out of the car and started CPR. At some point he dialed 911, and FHP and our road deputies responded."

"What time was this?"

He glanced at his watch. "About three or four hours ago."

"Any idea when the crash happened?"

"One of our patrol guys was out here about six hours ago, and the car wasn't here then."

I glanced down at the decomposing abdomen. It definitely didn't make sense, but I wasn't ready to concede that there was anything suspicious going on. I was looking for the simplest answer, but nothing was adding up.

"I think it's a staged scene," Lieutenant Tinnello said.

"A what?" This time, I think I actually *did* roll my eyes.

"I think someone staged this accident," he repeated. "I

think they rolled the car into the guardrail, placed her in the front seat, and took off."

I looked down at the body again. No marks. No bruising. No signs of trauma of any kind. There was some froth—a cone of foam—bubbling up from her nose and mouth, which is often consistent with a drug overdose. But that didn't mean it was suspicious. Lots of people get in wrecks because they're on drugs. And if she had overdosed, it would go a long way toward explaining why she'd coasted into the guardrail without braking or trying to avoid the crash to begin with.

"I think you're jumping to conclusions," I told him. "There's no evidence to suggest anything like that."

We debated the issue for a while longer, but neither the lieutenant nor I yielded our opinions on the matter. He was confident that the case was suspicious, and the scene was staged to look like an accident. I was adamant that the lieutenant's theory was a stretch of logic, and that he was simply being a typical cop. After a while the scene investigation was wrapped up, and the decedent was taken to the Medical Examiner's Office for autopsy.

Afterwards, my boss—the chief medical examiner—called me into his office. I took a seat on the other side of his desk as he opened the case folder and shoved my scene photographs over to me.

"Take a look at these photos, and tell me what's wrong with the story you gave in your report," he said.

I was nervous. I didn't like where this discussion was going at all. The doctor obviously had a 'teaching moment' for me, which meant I had gotten something horribly wrong.

"Did you find anything in the autopsy?" I asked, flipping through the photos.

"No injuries at all," he replied. "Now hush, and answer my question. What is off about these pictures?"

After a few minutes of scouring the images, it hit me like a slap to the face. I glanced up at him. I'm pretty sure my eyes told him everything he needed to know about my embarrassment.

"Well?" he asked. He wanted me to admit it.

Out loud.

"The lividity," I mumbled. "It's not right."

He smiled.

For those who don't know, lividity is the term used to describe where blood begins to pool in the body after the heart stops. With no heartbeat the blood stops flowing through veins and arteries, and basically is pulled down by gravity. The pooling of blood soaks into corpuscles near the skin, and turns the area of lividity a dark purple-ish color. After a while the blood congeals, and lividity is fixed. After that, no matter if a body is turned over or moved, the lividity stays put. With this, it's easy for a death investigator to tell if a body has been manipulated or moved at a scene.

Or, in this case, it could be used to tell whether a witness' statement was true or not.

"The guy who found the car said he found her leaning over the center console," I said. "But the lividity is concentrated on the left side of her face. That would suggest she was slumped over to the left—or the driver's side door." I point to a stream of dried purge that had come from her mouth, along with the froth I'd seen. "The purge is also moving to the left. She wasn't where the witness said she was."

"Exactly," the doctor said. "The sheriff's office detectives are right, I think. Given the fact that there are no injuries, and the inconsistency with her position in the car, I think this was a staged scene."

Sure enough, after further investigation by the sheriff's office, the full story became clear. The man who had supposedly found the car crash was pals with a friend of the decedent's. Apparently our victim's parents didn't like this friend, who often supplied her with drugs, and had threatened to kill the man if they ever caught the two of them together. As luck would have it, the night before, she had spent the evening with this friend. The two had done drugs, and she had died of an overdose.

Concerned about what her parents would do if they discovered the truth, the man had recruited the help of a buddy and the two staged the crash, placing her body into the driver's seat after pushing the car into the guardrail.

The detectives and lieutenant had been right all along. I had been horribly wrong. It was a lesson I would not soon forget.

Pride cometh…

Out of all the stories I've told in this book, this is the one, of course, of which I'm most embarrassed. How could I not be? It portrays me in a horrible light. It depicts me as arrogant and overconfident. Heck, now that I think about it, there're a few stories in this book that paint me this way—the times I tried to play Sherlock ring any bells?

That's one of the dangers experience brings to a person's life. It can make us difficult to work with. It can create a false sense of superiority toward those with less time in our particular field, or whose skills aren't quite honed to our standards. It fosters arrogance.

It bolsters pride.

And as King David would tell you, pride will always be our downfall. Or, more specifically, it "goes before destruction, and a haughty spirit before a fall" (Proverbs 16:18).

There's a popular Bible misquote that always makes me cringe when I hear it. It goes something like, "Money is the root of all evil." It's a misquote because the verse, written by the Apostle Paul, actually says, "For *the love of* money is the root of all *kinds of* evil" (1 Timothy 6:10, italics mine). Of course, Paul is tackling a specific issue here that young Timothy is facing in the church he's pastoring. If it wasn't a specific issue, I believe Paul would have delved deeper into the motivation of this 'love of money' which leads to various kinds of wrongdoing.

I believe he would have asked the question, "What drives a person to love money more than loving others?" To me, the answer would be that they love money because it can make their life easier. Better. More comfortable. To accumulate this money, at the expense of those less fortunate, shows a strong degree of self-interest. Perhaps selfishness. Extreme self-interest and selfishness, in my opinion, denotes a higher opinion of oneself. The person, in effect, places their own desires and comforts above those of the people around them. This seems to indicate a great deal of pride on their part.

But pride isn't just a root cause of a love of money or, to rephrase that, greed. Pride leads to so many other sins as well. I honestly have no qualms, in fact, with stating that pride might just be the root cause of all sin.

Think about it for a moment. What was the first sin? It

was when Lucifer rebelled against God in Heaven. Scripture tells us that Lucifer, who was deemed the most beautiful of all the angels, believed he could do a much better job running Heaven than God Himself. With this is mind, he orchestrated a rebellion with the intent of usurping the throne of God Almighty.

This rebellion, I believe, more than likely took place long before the creation of earth or humanity. I often see in literature or see on TV shows that Lucifer's rebellion occurred out of jealousy toward humanity. That he couldn't understand why mortal humans had such favor with God. But this, I think, is to create a sense of sympathy for him. We can all understand jealousy, can't we? We can understand sibling rivalry, and in many ways, humans and angels are siblings in that we're God's created beings. So, yeah...poor Lucifer. God just didn't understand where his mightiest archangel was coming from. He didn't understand poor Lucifer's broken heart over no longer being considered number one among creation.

Even if that were true—and I don't believe it is—the lesson is still the same. Whether Lucifer, the angel who would eventually become known to humanity as Satan or the devil, was motivated by a prideful sense of superiority to God Himself, or if jealousy of humanity spurred him on, it's still fueled by pride. Superiority and jealousy are two sides of the same coin. The coin of pride.

And Adam and Eve? Did they eat from the forbidden fruit because they were hungry? Not at all. They were allowed to eat from any of the trees in the Garden—and I imagine there were plenty—that they wanted to except from the Tree of Knowledge of Good and Evil. Did they eat from the forbidden tree because the fruit looked better than all the other fruit in the Garden? Well, the Bible indicates that the fruit was definitely pleasing to the eye, but that doesn't seem to be the reason either. After all, Eve doesn't even try to take a bite from it until the devil whispers a few sweet nothings in her ear.

"Go ahead," that old serpent said. "Eat that pretty little fruit. If you do, you'll be like God."

Like God.

That's the attitude of pride. It's placing ourselves far above anything and everything else. It's scooching God off His throne and plopping down in it ourselves, trying to make our own butt groove in the cushions.

Every sin we commit is a product of pride.

"Sure," we say to ourselves. "God told me not to do that, but I'm going to do it anyway...because, ya know, I want to."

That's essentially what we're saying when we commit a sin. We know it's wrong. But we just don't care. We do it anyway because we want to satisfy our own lusts...our own desires...or own sense of self-worth. When we sin God is removed from the equation in our minds, and only *we* exist in the universe.

That's what sin is. That's all that sin is. Putting ourselves above God. Pride.

I must decrease, so He will increase

John the Baptist is one of my all-time favorite figures in the Bible. He's someone I would have loved to meet in person, and yet someone I would have been terrified to meet in person. John, I imagine, cut a scary picture along that barren Galilean landscape.

Think about it.

He was a wild man. He literally lived in the wilderness. Dressed in furs. Was unruly and unkempt. His shoulders broad. His arms thick as trees. Hair and beard twisted and knotted. I imagine his voice carrying on the wind like thunder, shouting his message of the Messiah from the rooftops of the world. Oh, how his eyes must have seared into the hearts and souls of anyone who crossed paths with him.

He would have been a force to be reckoned with, so much so that, for the most part, the Sanhedrin left him alone. Kings gave him a wide berth. And people followed him in droves.

As preachers go he had Joel Osteen numbers, and while his message, too, was one of hope, it was built on the Word of God.

What a man of God. What a preacher.

I can imagine his charisma as being strong enough to have supported a great rebellion against the Romans if he had called for it. Heck, the people were already ready to take up arms with him. Many thought, by no fault of his own, that he was actually the Messiah himself. And to the people of that time, the Messiah was synonymous with throwing off the shackles of Roman rule and once again being a free Israel.

People believed this so much, in fact, that when they started hearing about this guy named Jesus they became concerned for their beloved leader, John. Jesus even had the audacity to steal John's very own ministry. He started baptizing people just like John. Worse, one day he started baptizing people in the very same region as John.

Concerned about this they approached John, warning him that there was someone out there—his very cousin, no less—who was threatening to usurp his mighty throne of influence. Jesus' numbers were growing. It was only a matter of time before some of John's flock would be switching sides. Only a matter of time before John's followers started abandoning him for that crazy carpenter from Nazareth.

"John," they said to him, "what are you going to do about your cousin? What are you going to do about Jesus?"

I can picture him now. His intense eyes twinkling as he lowered his massive form onto an overturned tree. Maybe a single tear trickled down his dirt-covered cheek as he looked over his concerned congregation. Oh, how he loved these people. Oh, what he wouldn't give to make them understand.

The crowd hushed as he cleared his throat. He took a pull from his water bladder, then wiped away the excess from his beard. Every eye was on him. No one wanted to breathe in case they might miss something really important at that moment.

He cleared his throat again. He'd been teaching and preaching so much that day already. His voice was hoarse. Maybe there was a slight tickle. The anticipation boiled among the crowd. They'd never seen him like this before. Was he at a loss for words?

They were sure it was all that Jesus' fault.

Finally, John the Baptist opened his mouth to speak. You could have heard a pin drop into the desert sand from two miles away. It was as if all of nature had gone silent for the words the great preacher was about to say.

"He must increase," John said. "I must decrease."

There was more to what the Baptizer said in John 3. But basically, that one sentence summed it all up. John's ministry had never been about himself. He had told them time and again that he was not the Messiah. He had preached constantly about the One who would come after him, the true Messiah. In that one simple sentence, he was making it clear. Jesus was the One.

In essence, he was telling his followers, "My work is finished. I've been pointing to Jesus all along. There He is, over there, baptizing people. I baptize with water. He baptizes with Heavenly, cleansing fire."

The only way for Jesus to truly shine in this world was for John to take a step back. "Don't follow me," he was saying. "Follow Jesus."

Here he was...probably the greatest preacher in human history. The crowds adored him. They would have marched into Hell itself if he told them to do so. And he bowed down to his cousin.

Think about that. It would be one thing if Jesus had been a stranger. It would have been something else if Jesus had been someone John had never met, but knew from divine revelation that Jesus was truly God's son. Instead, John had probably grown up with Him. He'd played ball in the backyard with Him. They'd pushed each other on swing sets at the park. John knew Jesus like very few others had ever known Him.

Think about your own cousin. Your own brother or sister. Your own family member. No matter how much you may love them, would you be willing to give up your prestige for them? Would you be willing to relinquish your influence to them? There's something very human about sibling rivalry—and it's always centered on pride. We don't like submitting, no matter how close to someone we may be. We always want to be king of the mountain. We always want to be the team captain. We always want to be leader of the pack.

That's pride, too.

But John? He didn't even hesitate. He probably nodded out toward the river where Jesus was busy baptizing new followers, smiled, and said, "He's the one you seek. I've just been pointing the way. Now go to Him."

There was no pride there. There was nothing but submission. Humility. Loyalty. And, most importantly, love. Not just love for God and his cousin, Jesus. But love for his followers as well. A sort of love that put them far ahead of his own desires for greatness.

"I must decrease. He must increase."

Jesus is the one you want, but to follow Him we must tamp down the pride that swells in our chests and sticks out from our chins. To follow Him, we must submit ourselves. To follow Him we must decrease, so that He can increase our lives in abundance.

16

NINE TOXIC LIVES

CASE # 10-0102
DECEDENT: REDACTED, Clint
Re: Asphyxia

"Get out!" Jennifer shouted, shoving her boyfriend Clint toward the door.

His feet dug into the carpet, refusing to be moved.

"Come on, Jen. Stop being so dramatic!"

They'd been arguing for hours, but Jennifer just couldn't let it go this time. She was sick and tired of Clint's drinking, and it was time to put her foot down.

"I'm the one being dramatic?" She pushed against his chest again. "You were the one outside, screaming at our neighbors like some dying cat. You get this way every time your drink."

It wasn't the only issue she had with his drinking, either. Last time he got like this he had cheated on her with Gloria

Gossett, her former best friend. It had taken some time to get over it, and even now she didn't fully trust him because of it.

"Come on, baby. Don't kick me out again." He stumbled backwards. He was having trouble even standing upright, he was so intoxicated. "I'll be good. I promise."

His words slurred.

"No. I told you last time, I wouldn't put up with another bender like this." She shoved him toward the door again. "Get out!"

This time, he couldn't contain his balance. He fell back, onto the floor. His legs wobbled in the air as he struggled to sit up. When he finally did, his eyes narrowed. His brow creased.

He cursed, then stood up and swung his fist at her. If he was less intoxicated, the blow would have found its mark and it would have been Jennifer on the ground this time.

That's it.

She left him teetering at the front door, dashed into the bedroom and returned a few moments later, hefting a Louisville Slugger baseball bat. Clint's eyes widened as they finally focused on what she was holding.

"You're never going to put your hands on me again!" she screamed, raising the bat in the air.

"Okay. Okay!" he shouted, holding up his hands. "I'll go."

With that, he turned around and stumbled out the door.

It was seven in the morning, and I pulled up to the nice little double-wide trailer in the middle of the boondocks. I'd gotten the call around 5:30 that morning, and it had taken me nearly an hour to drive all the way out to the scene. I wasn't happy. I'm a night owl. Early morning call-outs are never fun for me...especially on nights when I don't fall asleep until about two or three.

It was a cold February morning, too. Yeah, even in Florida we have those. The big difference is we're not as accustomed to them, so I shivered as I climbed out of my car and walked up to the detectives huddled near the front of the house.

"So what's the story?" I asked the group.

Detective Conrad looked up from the steaming cup of coffee clutched in her hands, and smiled. From the looks of things she was just as tired as me, but was putting on a brave face.

"The couple who lives here were arguing last night," she told me. "It got heated. He'd been drinking. A lot. And during the heat of the moment, he tried to hit her."

Oh, I could see where this was going. Domestic violence. Fits of passion. I waited for her to continue.

"The girlfriend then grabbed a baseball bat and..."

"Don't tell me," I said. "She beat him to death."

The other detectives in the group chuckled. They weren't being insensitive. It was just that I wasn't even close.

Conrad shook her head. "Not exactly. In fact, when she grabbed the bat, he left. Voluntarily."

She motioned for me to follow her, and we started walking around the mobile home's property toward the back.

"He left the house," she continued as we walked, "but he didn't leave the property. Instead he spent all night outside, banging on the door, begging to come inside."

Goosebumps rippled down my arms from a cold chill blowing in from the ocean.

"Ah, geez," I said. "Don't tell me the guy froze to death out here."

With a slight smile, she shook her head. "No, nothing like that." We stopped walking just before turning the corner to the side of the house. "After a while, the girlfriend finally went to bed. She turned on the radio to drown out his voice and banging on the door, and fell asleep. This morning she woke up, went to the kitchen to make breakfast, and found him."

At that, she gestured for me to walk around the side of the house. I followed her silent command, and noticed a small wooden porch leading to a white side door.

I blinked when I saw it. I wasn't sure I was seeing what my brain was telling me I was looking at. I looked again. Blinked. A set of feet and legs lay lifeless on the porch.

Slowly I walked up the steps, letting my eyes trace the outline of the body. It seemed to disappear at the waist.

Then, I noticed the cat door. It was no taller than ten inches, and maybe five or six inches wide. A tiny, tiny cat door.

And my victim's upper torso—from the waist up—was crammed inside, nice and cozy in the heated kitchen on the other side of the door. He was, of course, undeniably dead.

It seems that sometime during the night, when Clint realized his girlfriend wasn't going to open the house up to him again, he decided to take matters into his own hands. He decided to get clever. He was a thin guy. Tall, but very slender. He must have walked around the house...maybe a few times...trying to think of some way to get inside. He must have seen the cat door and thought he was thin enough to squeeze through. And it had almost worked. He managed to slip halfway through with no problem. Then, the worst possible thing happened.

He got stuck. He couldn't go forward. He couldn't back

out. He was trapped.

Plus, the space was so tight, he couldn't breathe either. He died there. No telling how long it took, but he died there of asphyxia. He couldn't breathe. His body slowly shut down. And he died halfway into the house he so desperately wanted to be in.

Suffocation

I honestly hadn't planned on sharing this lesson for this book if I'm honest. I'm uncomfortable talking about it. Not because it's controversial or a difficult subject to broach, but because entire volumes could be written about it and not even scratch the surface of the subject. Another reason I was hesitant to discuss this topic is because, as a teacher of God's word, I have a responsibility to speak the truth and not sugar coat things, no matter how unpopular what I'm going to say might be. And frankly, I just wanted to write an interesting book with a unique perspective on God and having a wonderfully abundant life.

But the truth is, there is no wonderfully abundant life if we find ourselves stuck in a toxic relationship with someone who suffocates the joy from our lives. Such relationships slowly kill us. They wrapped their gnarled fingers around our throats, and slowly squeeze until the life drains from us.

Just like that little cat door.

Don't get me wrong, in the above case the guy wasn't innocent. He was, by all accounts, the toxic influence in the relationship. But I think the lesson is still there.

We must avoid toxic relationships at all costs if we want to thrive. If we want to have joy in our lives. If we want to experience that incredible life that Christ has in store for us.

Choose Wisely

Ever see *Indiana Jones and the Last Crusade*? Not many people haven't. Remember the end? Indy and the Nazi stand there in that ancient cavern. They're given a choice of goblets to drink water from. Among the horde of precious, jewel-encrusted goblets, the one and only Holy Grail sits. The old knight tells them, "You must choose. But choose wisely."

The idea is that they were to pick one of the hundreds of goblets, fill it with water, then drink. If they chose correctly, they would be healed of any ailments they might have. If those chose wrong...well, it wouldn't be good.

The Nazi villain found out the hard way. He chose the most beautiful. He chose the most royal-looking. He chose the most eye-pleasing goblet of the whole set. "Surely, this is the cup of the King of Kings," he says. He drinks from it, and in a series of cinematic special effects he dries up into a husk. His life is drained away, and he crumples to the floor in a heap of bone and dust.

"He chose poorly," the old Templar knight says.

The Nazi had picked the cup of a king, and not that of a humble carpenter. He'd chosen superficially. He'd chosen a treasure of great financial value. He'd chosen what tickled his sense of the aesthetic, and had never even considered the quality of the goblet. Never considered what was on the inside. Never bothered to look at the non-material worth of the cup.

This next part is basically for single people, looking for love. I'll get to you married lot in a few minutes. But it wouldn't hurt for everyone to pay attention to what I'm about to say, married or not.

All too often, when choosing our mates, we process that choice in a similar fashion. We look at how much they appeal to our sense of beauty or attractiveness. There's nothing wrong with that on the surface. I think God definitely makes people attractive to each other with the intent of bringing them together initially. The problem is, many of us stop there. They're attractive. Let's jump into a relationship together.

And after a while their inner qualities begin to shine through, and we discover they're toxic. They're slowly poisoning us. We feel our joy and happiness drying up . Maybe we even find ourselves in pain—physically, emotionally, spiritually, or all of the above.

Get rid of them.

"But Kent, I love him."

"You don't understand, Kent. She's the world to me."

And I'll repeat myself. Get rid of them.

You will not know joy. You will not know peace. You will not enjoy this precious thing called life if you hold on to these toxic people. Get rid of them, wipe your hands of them, and next time choose wisely. Go deeper before moving into a relationship with them. It's unwise for a toad to fall in love with a serpent. They're incompatible. The snake will eat the toad every time.

Trust me. I know this better than anyone. I've been in such a relationship before. I met a woman of exquisite worldly beauty. Didn't bother to really get to know her. I didn't love her, but lusted after her. I made excuse after excuse after excuse for her, and refused to let her go. After a while, it became a matter of principle for me to stay with her. She had some good qualities. Surely, she would change after a while. If she truly loved me, surely she would change for me. Right?

But as the relationship continued, her grip around my throat continued to tighten. She drove a wedge between my family and me. She pushed my friends away. I fell away from the church. I started drinking alcohol to cope—not much, mind you. Never enough to get drunk. Just enough to ease the tension. But if you're forced to take a sip of alcohol just to fall asleep at night, that relationship is toxic. That relationship was killing me.

Eventually, I got rid of her. But not before I had lost my job. Not before I had done severe damage to lifelong relationships with friends and family. Not before I had been stripped of the life I had worked so hard to build for myself.

In a toxic relationship? Get rid of them. Now. Don't wait.

You owe it to yourself. You owe it to your future mate. You owe it to the God of the universe to live the wondrous, abundant life He has in mind for you.

Get rid of him. Get rid of her. Before you find yourself struggling for breath, halfway in and halfway out of the place you want to be.

Married folks?

This is really the part of this lesson that I've dreaded. The reason I've dreaded it is because there are no easy answers to a toxic marriage. I can't honestly tell you to "get rid of him" or "get rid of her", as easily as I'm able to tell the single people. Truth is, you're married. And marriage is a sacred covenant. It's a covenant not just between you and your spouse, but with you, your spouse, and God.

It's not as easy as saying, "Just get a divorce."

The reason it's not easy to say—at least for me—is because I struggle with this question myself. No one would deny that God doesn't like divorce. After all, marriage is a symbolic picture of His relationship with the Church. His relationship with Christians. His relationship with you and with me. And since He went to great pains to ensure that once we're saved, we're always saved—He'll never divorce us—then for Christians to so easily discard their spouses is to mock one of the most amazing things about God's grace.

So what happens if your marriage is toxic? What happens if your spouse is abusive? Doesn't He want us to be happy? Safe?

I hate to be the bearer of such a truth, but He never promised believers a safe life. He never promised us a comfortable life. He never promised us happiness. Abundant life is not synonymous with a happy life. In fact, time and again in Scripture, it's made clear that to follow Him, things are going to be tough. We're not living our lives anymore. We've given our lives over to Him, and therefore His will trumps our own. Sometimes, that's going to be uncomfortable. Sometimes, that's going to be painful even.

This is why it's so important for us to choose our mates wisely *before* we devote ourselves to marrying them. This is why it's essential that we are highly selective when we look for the person we will spend the rest of our lives with.

It's not that God doesn't want you to be happy. He really

doesn't want you to suffer through a miserable marriage. But before we choose that person, we should first be sure.

But what if you were married before coming to know Christ?

See? That's why I was reluctant to talk about this. I just don't have the answers, and I'm not going to make something up to sell a book. This is where I'll soundly tell you, if you're in this situation consult your pastor. But don't readily accept what he says on the subject either. Do your own research. Read your Bible. Search for the answers. Pray. These are the ways a mature Christian discerns answers to the questions they seek.

1 Corinthians 7 seems to provide the only acceptable reason for divorce in Scripture. Verse 15 states, "But if the unbeliever (spouse) leaves, let it be so. The brother or the sister is not bound in such circumstances; God has called us to live in peace." This verse seems to indicate that if an unbeliever wishes to divorce a believer, it is acceptable to do so. It appears to be the only place in the Bible that allows for such an action.

But the same chapter also states that if the unbeliever is content to live with the believer, the believer should stay in the marriage. The reason for this is that there is always hope that our own faith in Christ can transform our spouses into believers as well.

Everyone's situation is different. I think that's why Scripture isn't as clear-cut on the subject of divorce as other theological topics.

Truth is, I'm divorced.

Whether it was a sin for me to divorce my wife or not, I'm not sure. But I also haven't married again, which seems to be the biggest issue in the Bible concerning the topic. Most of the time, when the subject of divorce comes up it seems to be connected with marrying again, and whether or not it is adultery or polygamy. I haven't married again. I don't believe I will marry again. I'm fine with that. (My parents...not so much.)

But this is one of those life-changing decisions that only you can decide. Only you know if it's something you should do, and whether you are okay with the consequences it brings.

Live a toxin-free life

Whether you're single or married, or somewhere in between, there's no doubt of one thing—we must rid ourselves of the toxins in our relationships if we ever hope to have an abundant life. The key is discovering how to do so.

In some situations, it is as simple as removing the toxic person from our lives. Be brave. Be strong. Do it, if you're dating, courting, or are engaged to such a person. Don't let them steal your abundant life. Don't let them squeeze the life from you.

If you're married, and don't feel divorce is the answer, find a way to deal with the toxic environment. Seek help. Reach out to your ministry team. Counseling. Family and friends. In extreme circumstances, remove yourself from the environment for as long as you need. (I would never suggest you remain in a dangerous situation.)

But if you ever hope to have a joy-filled, abundant life, do whatever it takes to deal with bad relationships.

17

BLOOD SPATTER

This next story isn't really a case. As a matter of fact, I wasn't even working as a forensic death investigator at the time. I had taken a break from the job and was now at seminary, working on my master's degree. One of the required classes for my program was an evangelism class, and as part of that class we were required to do the unthinkable. We were required to pair off into teams of three, drive out to the farthest reaches of the area in which we lived, go up to complete strangers' houses, and share the gospel of Jesus Christ.

I know, right? Scary stuff.

If you're not a Christian, and you've always wondered about this, let me set the record straight. Nobody likes doing it. It's awkward, not only for the stranger, but also for the would-be evangelists. No one likes going up to people out of the blue and reciting some car salesman spiel to try to convince someone to accept Christ as their Lord and Savior. (NOTE: Before you get the wrong idea, Christians are most definitely tasked by the Great Commission (Matthew 28:18-20) to share the good news of Christ to the world. I personally think we've been doing it wrong for a long time now. What we are not called to do—and shouldn't be trying to do—is convince anyone of that good news. God can handle the convincing all by Himself.)

Anyway, back to the tale.

As I was saying, I had teamed up with two other seminary students and had driven out to a very rural area in North Carolina to do 'cold call' evangelism. It was the dead of winter. Winds were high, and cut through our clothing like a lightsaber through an old Jedi's robes. It was drizzling rain, and the forecast called for snow flurries. None of my team were exceptionally happy to be out there that day, but we were determined to give it our best shot. Not for the grade, but because we really wanted to see God do something amazing through us.

We came across a low-rent trailer park, and decided to give the place a try. We parked our car near the entrance of the park, and started walking door to door. The outcome was predictable. The majority of people hardly opened their doors to us. The few who did only peeked through the crack long enough to tell us they weren't interested. After about an hour, our limbs felt stiff from near freezing temperatures and our hearts were heavy from our perceived failure.

We decided to give it just a little more time. One or two more trailers, and we would call it a day.

The very next place we knocked was a welcome change of pace, however. The door opened up, and an elderly black woman looked out at us. Concern was on her face. She was wary of why three white people were at her door in such nasty weather. But she'd been raised to be polite. She'd been raised to be hospitable. When we told her who we were, even though she made it clear she wasn't interested, she invited us inside to get warm. I can't tell you how appreciative I was for her upbringing at that moment.

We stepped into the dark interior of her home. It was sparse, but tidy. There was a distinct stench of mildew permeating the air, but I could tell she took great pains to clean what she could. She didn't wait for us once we entered. Instead, she weaved her way through the kitchen and into the living room without asking us to join her. We followed her anyway, and found her already reclining in her La-Z-Boy with a remote in hand and watching television.

I felt so uncomfortable. I felt like I was intruding. Like I was being rude for just being there. She clearly didn't want us there, and was only trying to be polite in the most legalistic sense of the word. She offered us nothing to drink or eat. And she clearly had no interest in talking with us. I contemplated motioning to our team that we should leave, but we had made it inside. She was a captive audience, in a way. It would be a shame to leave without at least trying to tell her about Jesus while we had the opportunity.

So, taking deep breaths to calm our nerves and garner our courage, we started talking. We went through the talking points of the gospel. We told her about how we're all sinners, and because of that cannot have a relationship with the God who created us. We explained how God loves us so much, He decided to fix our relationship by sending Christ into the world to take our sin and our punishment. We shared how all we had to do was trust Jesus, make Him Lord of our lives, and we could have that relationship with God that makes us whole.

Blood Spatter | 169

We were on fire. We were sharing our hearts out. We were passionate and sincere.

And it all fell on deaf ears. Her attention was solely focused on the television in front of us. She hadn't even offered a nod in our direction. It was clear she wanted nothing to do with our message. She wanted nothing to do with us. She just wanted to watch her programs in peace.

Defeated, I thought I might join her. I turned my attention to the TV and started watching it with her. Then, I realized what she was watching, and it literally felt like a light bulb must have been hovering over my head. I couldn't believe my luck. I couldn't believe this was happening. And I knew, without a doubt, it had nothing at all to do with luck. This was the 'God moment' we'd been hoping for.

She was watching reruns of the hit television show *CSI*.

After a few moments a commercial break came on, and I seized the opportunity.

"You like *CSI*?" I asked.

Her eyes darted from the TV to me for a split second, and she offered a quick nod. I also noticed a quick smile on her face as she did so.

So, this woman didn't just like the show. She loved it.

"I used to do that for a living," I told her.

Her eyes widened as she heard this, and she turned to look at me. "Really?"

I nodded. "Yep. I worked for a medical examiner's office in Florida. I was a forensic investigator and went to crime scenes. I've done a lot of the things they do on *CSI*."

Now she was all ears. The show had returned after the commercial, but she was no longer interested. Instead, she started talking to me about the job. In return I answered her questions enthusiastically, sharing many of the same stories

I've talked about in this book. I told her how the job was different from TV, but also where the shows got it right, too. She took it all in with a huge smile on her face. And still she asked questions.

I'm not sure how long we talked, but I know one episode ended and another had begun again before I began steering the conversation back to where I wanted it to be.

"What's your favorite part about *CSI*?" I asked her, genuinely curious.

Her eyes narrowed as she considered the question for a few minutes. Then she broke out into a grin. "I suppose it's when they look at blood splatter and stuff, and can tell where someone was struck in a room and then reconstruct the crime from it all," she said. "Uh-huh...that's it. I always like when they do that."

I couldn't contain my own smile. Her joy at discussing her favorite show was contagious. I really liked this woman. She had such wondrous passion for it all. It was almost childlike how much she obviously loved it.

"I'm fascinated with blood spatter, too," I told her. "I've even taken a few courses on it."

"Really?" Her eyes were as big as saucers now.

I nodded.

"Blood spatter is really amazing," I said. "The whole thing is just crazy. Imagine. A killer murders someone, and blood gets everywhere."

She started nodding, indicating she was following what I was saying.

"I mean, it's everywhere. It's on the floor. It's on the ceiling. It's all over the walls. And that blood just stains whatever it touches." I hadn't thought this through at all. It was flowing from the lips as fast as my brain thought it up. I silently prayed that it would make sense when it was over. "So the killer gets rid of the body. Finds the perfect place to bury it. But now he's got a problem."

"The splatter," she said. "The blood is everywhere."

I grinned. "Exactly. Body is gone, but the blood is everywhere. To get away with his crime, he's got to get rid of it. So, he gets cleaning supplies—a mop and floor cleaner—and he starts trying to clean it up."

She nodded excitedly. The woman really did love this stuff.

"But the cleaning supplies aren't enough. He got much of it up, but it's left stains that no amount of soap and water can get out. So what does he do?"

She thought about it a moment, then blurted, "Bleach!"

"That's right! He gets bleach. He uses the bleach, and even more of it comes out. Unfortunately, not enough. The stains are still visible. He can still be implicated in the crime."

I knew where I was going now, but I had no idea where the idea was coming from. I'm not this clever. It could only be coming from God.

"So this killer, who thinks he's smarter than the police, decides he'll get rid of the evidence once and for all. He goes and buys a bunch of paint. Comes back to the scene of the crime, and paints the whole house...top to bottom. He even goes the extra mile, and applies two coats everywhere." I was smiling from ear to ear. I'm loving this now. "But guess what?"

"What?"

"The killer isn't aware of this, but that blood isn't gone. Covered up, yes. But not gone. So the crime scene investigator comes in and he's got this special light—an alternate light source. He shines that light around the crime scene, and after using some chemicals sprayed over the walls and floor the blood stains shine like a full moon in that room. And the killer is caught because of it."

The look on her face was priceless. She loved my little story. My parable, if you will.

"You know what? That's just like us."

The smile on her face faded just a hint, but I could tell she wanted to see where I was going with this. So I pressed on.

"Our lives are stained with sin, just like that crime scene was stained with blood spatter," I explained. "We try to clean it up ourselves, but the stains remain. We try to get clever and cover it up, but in the perfect light of God those stains are revealed for the whole world to see."

Her mouth dropped open. She'd heard me. She'd understood.

"However, unlike that murderer, we have a great advocate in Jesus. He's not only our defense, but He's also a great carpenter. If we ask him to, He'll come in and tear down those old sin-stained walls. There'll no longer be any evidence to convict us. We're guilty, there's no doubt. But Jesus will take care of the evidence for us. Not only will He tear down those stained walls, but He'll build us brand new, stain-resistant walls. Walls that, even though we might continue to sin, will never be stained again. And He guarantees His craftsmanship...His handiwork."

She was speechless. She wasn't disinterested, like she had been in the beginning. But now, I could tell she was really thinking about what I'd just told her. She'd heard the gospel. She knew the good news of Jesus Christ. And now, it was between her and Christ as to what she would do with that news.

At the end of that chance meeting, she wasn't quite ready to trust in Christ. But as I said, it's not our job to convince. It's just our job to share what we know. Share what Jesus has done for us. Be truthful as to how He's changed us. We're not supposed to 'win' them. We're not supposed to beat them over the head with the gospel. We're supposed to trust that God will take care of the rest.

I have no idea what happened to that wonderful, sweet lady. I pray that one day the truth of what I had shared with her finally came home to roost, and she trusted Christ as her Lord and Savior. I pray that with all my heart. But I guess I'll only find out when we're all together again in Heaven, and I'm fine with that. I'm just thankful that God used me in that moment —used something I knew like the back of my hand to reach out to a woman who would have never listened otherwise.

Whether or not she ever gets saved, that little encounter changed everything for me. It changed how I viewed evangelism. It changed how I shared my faith. It gave me a deep passion for evangelism. And it taught me the most vital thing of all—trust God to do His work.

Trust God

If there's one thing this book teaches you about how to live an abundant life, I hope it is this: Trust God. That one little bit of advice will take care of all the rest. Have a problem and don't know how to deal with it?

Trust God.

That old saying, "God helps those who helps themselves" is not in the Bible. Do your own search. You won't find it anywhere. In fact, it's quite the opposite. God wants us to rely on Him for every aspect of our lives, no matter how big or how small.

That problem that seems so daunting to you? It's child's play to God. What's more, it's more than likely part of His plan. Trust Him to take care of it.

Mounting financial troubles?

Well, there are a few things you can do to take care of that, but in the meantime don't lose heart. Trust God. He'll provide for you.

Have you received bad news? Maybe a bad medical diagnosis?

Trust your doctors, but more than that...trust God. He's the Great Physician. He brought dead people to life, even though the thought of that in my job might freak me out a bit. He made the deaf able to hear. He gave sight to the blind, and cured lepers. Just the touch from the hem of his garment cured a woman who couldn't stop her bleeding. God heals. Trust Him.

Having troubles on the job?

He's got that covered, too.

Point is, if you want to have a joy-filled abundant life...if you want to live a life beyond your wildest dreams...let go and let God.

He's there for you. He can handle it all. And if you're not worried about all the little and big things life throws at you, you'll have much more time to enjoy it. Trust in Him.

"Trust in the Lord with all your heart and lean not on

your own understanding; in all your ways submit to him, and he will make your paths straight." (Proverbs 3:5-6)

Want an abundant life? Trust God. He's the master of straightening out those rough shoulders and curving highways. Trust in Him, and enjoy the ride.

ABOUT THE AUTHOR

Bestselling author J. Kent Holloway lives on death. Literally. With more than twenty-four years' experience in forensic death investigations, he's seen it all. Experienced the worst that life has to give and never let it dim his sense of wonder or humor. Now, he brings all this experience, along with a zeal for uncovering the folklore and superstitions of death, to the written page as author of mysteries, forensic crime fiction, paranormal thrillers, and Christian fiction and nonfiction!

He is the author of the highly acclaimed Ezekiel Crane paranormal mystery series, as well as some of his more traditional mysteries, KILLYPSO ISLAND and the forensic thriller, CLEAN EXIT. He's even started a series wherein Death himself takes on the role of sleuth in the witty and twisty DEATH WARMED OVER.

Kent Holloway also has a Master's degree in Biblical Studies from Southeastern Baptist Theological Seminary. He has served as singles minister, evangelism pastor, and director of discipleship and education.

You can learn more about him by visiting his website at www.kenthollowayonline.com.

www.ingramcontent.com/pod-product-compliance
Lightning Source LLC
Chambersburg PA
CBHW021950290426
44108CB00012B/1011